MW00791514

THE POWER OF MENTORSHIP

Don Boyer

Real Life Teaching/Publishing
donboyer@realifeteaching.com

THE POWER OF MENTORSHIP

Published by Real Life Teaching/Publishing
donboyer@realifeteaching.com
562-789-1909
Whittier, California

Cover Design by Justin Spina
jspina@mediawestproductions.com

Editor, Composition, and Typography by Janet Althouse
AlthouseWords@aol.com

Photos by Vics Magsaysay
vicsmag@yahoo.com

This book is available at quantity discounts for bulk purchase.
For more information contact:
Real Life Teaching/Publishing
donboyer@realifeteaching.com
562-789-1909
Whittier, California

Printed in the United States of America

Foreword

"In the end…the extent of our own success will be measured by the accomplishments we have helped create in others." That is what mentorship is all about. It's about realizing success by helping others achieve their goals.

What you are about to read are some incredible stories that remind us of the famous Ziglar quote: "You can have anything you desire in life as long as you are willing to help enough other people get what they want first." The true secret to great abundance is to assist others along the way.

What Don Boyer has done is bring together a wealth of masterminds who have opened up their hearts and vaults of information to you. The stories they share are from real life experiences and are commonsense truths that, when applied, can result in enormous prosperity.

Within these golden pages, you will discover lessons that have not been told, as well as proven, time-tested principles that can help anyone who's ever asked, "How can I get more out of life?" While you absorb these messages, please understand one thing, information is just that, until it is applied into action.

Mr. Boyer has compiled these authors for a very certain purpose. He understands the power that each of these individuals holds, and he challenges you, the reader, to not only consume these insights, but to actually put them into motion for yourself.

If it is your mission to find a mentor, then use these stories as your beacon to guide you to your destiny. And if it is your passion to help others, then by all means utilize these passages to encourage you to find your pupil.

One of the great philosophers once said, "When the student is ready, the teacher appears." Let this book serve as evidence that that time is now. Just the fact that you are reading this demonstrates that you are ready to take that next step toward a brighter tomorrow, for yourself as well as someone else.

With that said, reading is not enough. Once you have finished this book, both Don and I would like to challenge you to do something special—take action and fulfill your promise of making a difference in this world.

For, "the greatest success we'll know is helping others succeed and grow."

Best wishes and what ever you do…

Keep smilin'……….

Gregory Scott Reid, #1 bestselling author of *The Millionaire Mentor, Positive Impact,* and *Wake Up—Live the Life You Love.* www.MisterKeynote.com

Dedication

To all the Champions who have the courage to follow their dreams, pursue their vision, and step out in faith while facing fear and overcoming it!

We dedicate this book also to all those who are living life with passion, who understand the importance of mentorship, and have dedicated their lives to mentor others. You are the ones who achieve your dreams and not just dream about achievement.

Acknowledgments

First and foremost, I want to thank my Lord and Savior Jesus Christ for He gave me life and life more abundantly. This gift allows me to use my talent and skills to their fullest potential.

To Melinda Boyer for being the best wife any man could ask for. Your faithfulness and commitment is beyond price. Thank you for always being in my corner.

To all our children and grandchildren who give me the drive and staying power to move on my dreams in order to have them feel proud of their dad and grandpa by being one who was faithful to his calling.

To all the authors in this book who were willing to step out in faith, to share their wisdom, experience, time, and money to help make life better for all those who read this book. I am truly honored and humbled to be in association with each and every one of you and to call you my friends. It is your faith, integrity, and courage displayed by co-authoring this book that makes you all champions of champions.

To Greg S. Reid who has gone far above the call of duty as my mentor. For the time spent with me to guide me to the next level of business and personal success, I am deeply grateful. Thank you for always being there when I need direction. You truly are "The Millionaire Mentor."

To Wil Cason, a true friend, who was put into my life by Divine design—thank you for inspiring me to move forward and follow my passion, vision, and dreams. You did this verbally, and in writing, but most of all by example.

To Janet Althouse, for taking on this project and providing the professional image to create a dynamic book—your skills as an editor have been a true gift and blessing to us. Thank you for all your help and the endless hours you put into making this a book we can all be proud to put our names on.

To Justin Spina—thank you for using your gift and talent designing the book cover. It is a master piece! It was wonderful working with you. Your design contribution is helping our book become a bestseller.

And to my closest and dearest friend, Mel Brodsky, who not only acts as a mentor and business partner, but is the one who gave me my first start in this wonderful field of personal growth and development. I truly call him "Partner."

Introduction

Mentors hold the golden key to unleash your potential and unlock your future. Wow! What a powerful statement; not because it sounds good, but because it is the foundation of all success and achievement. Whatever level of success you have achieved thus far in your life has been due to some type of mentor. Whether that mentor was in person, or in the form of books, tapes, and seminars, you were given the knowledge that took you from where you were to where you are right now.

To further this line of truth, in order to go from where you are currently to where you desire to be, it will take the insight, wisdom, and knowledge of a mentor. Your mentors are dedicated to helping you reach all of your dreams and goals and help pull out your full potential. Millions of people live far below their potential, because they do not seek a mentor to help them develop all of their abilities.

A mentor can see your greatness sitting there inside of you ready to come out, when all you can see are roadblocks and dead-ends. A mentor exists in order to guide you to the next level of success you desire. A mentor is not designed to nag you, baby sit you, or do your job for you. No, mentors are there to support your dreams, guide you past the pitfalls, point you in the right direction, and give you the knowledge to get the job done.

Mentors are a true rare breed of champions that bring to the table every type of experience, knowledge, wisdom, insight, and teaching style. Some are patient and kind, others direct and forceful, but the common denominator they all have is they are dedicated to improving your life. Why would multi-millionaires who have fame continue to travel, speak, coach, and write? Because they are true mentors, that is what they were designed to do.

Mentors have unleashed my potential and unlocked my future, and that is why I am so excited to bring you this powerful book on mentorship. I have sought out some of the best mentors of our time, and put them into a format so that they can help you to reach any level of success you want, attain any goal you set for yourself, and sharpen your skills. They will share with you what success is really all about— it is a journey and process not found in one set of plans or steps. Success is a personal event, meaning different things to different people.

This being the case, what ever your definition of success and achievement, you will find a mentor within these pages to help you achieve it. Based on proven track records, every one of these mentors has proven themselves to excel in their area of expertise. It is my desire, as well as every mentor in this book, that you reach every goal and dream you have and find the ultimate level of success that is right for you. In return—you go out and mentor others!

Don Boyer

Contents

Foreword by Gregory Scott Reid

Meet Your Mentors
By Don Boyer

Let me personally introduce you to your inner circle of mentors. These men and women have proven themselves in their area of specialty to be the industry's top entrepreneurs, millionaires, thinkers, coaches, and trainers. You will enjoy their humor and gain powerful insights from their experience and wisdom, helping you to bring out your full potential, find your purpose, and live with passion.

So, if you are ready, let me introduce you to…

The legendary William E. Bailey, the mentor of mentors. The man Jim Rohn and Les Brown call teacher. Mr. Bailey has lived an extraordinary life that includes having a personal meeting with the Pope, having lunch with Neil Armstrong 6 months after he returned from the moon, and building a network marketing company that, in its peak, produced $64 million dollars a month.

He has flown his own personal corporate jet, sailed his 110-foot yacht, and helped many people become multimillionaires. This is a man who can help you climb the millionaire mountain.

Let's stroll over here and meet Mr. Carmelo Flores—a champion this young man. A self-made millionaire, with a rich background in real estate, and a successful business owner, he is a leading speaker and trainer in the area of personal and business development. His savvy, wisdom, and insight allowed him to join the millionaire membership group, leading his company to record breaking growth. He is a mentor who can help lead you to the top. He has personally helped me reach my next level of success, and his goal setting system is one of the best programs on the market. In this book, Carmelo mentors you on that system.

Over here, let's meet Mr. David Diaz. This young man is not only a smart and savvy businessman, but with his handsome dress and composure, he looks like he should be in a Hollywood Movie! With his sharp image, David has traveled all over the world, including China, Korea, Italy, Cambodia, and England, speaking and conducting business internationally. Professional speaking and being on the cutting edge of business in the 21st Century allows him the opportunity to be a frequent guest on television and radio. His experience and knowledge can help bring out the best in you.

Now here is Glen Curry—a mentor who has extraordinary insights on how to get things done. He is the author of numerous bestselling books and CDs as well as having a very successful daily radio show. His teaching and writing skills have a wonderful way of taking the laws of success and achievement and putting them in an easy-to-understand format. You will love his chapter as he shares one of the most powerful secrets to success which is…well go over to his chapter! He is waiting for you there and will tell you all about it.

And this is Mr. Jerry Haines. Talk about wisdom and insight! This is a mentor who has traveled and worked with what some believe to be the most prominent philosopher of our time, Mr. Jim Rohn. Jerry Haines, a millionaire himself, knows and understands the dynamics of how to turn wealth from a dream into reality. He will be sharing with you some powerful secrets that he himself personally learned from his own mentor. What a treat to be able to tap into his wealth of wisdom and insight. He is a living example of—"If you have a dream...you can turn it into a reality."

Let's go over here and bask in some "Sunshine". That is the nickname of our next mentor, Melinda Boyer. With wit and humor, she will help you understand the benefits and challenges of being married to a leader. Leaders are a rare breed indeed—sometimes they are wonderful gifts from above, other times you want to put them on a curb with a sign that reads "Will pay $100 to take off my hands!" She shares with ladies that being married to a leader means being a partner with their calling. A true leader cannot turn on and off his calling; therefore, it takes extreme wisdom and insight to make this partnership a successful venture.

Do you want to know how to keep going when your going got up and left? Meet Pete Urueta—I call him Mr. Persistence. If this guy had a banner over his head, it would read "Never Give Up!" Pete is an outstanding business man with insights on how to keep going when life and business feel like you are in the middle of the desert with no water. Pete knows the secrets how to keep going until you find your oasis. You will love his insight and wisdom.

Hey, look at this next crowd of championship mentors...

Mel Brodsky, or better known as Millionaire Mel, has been one of my personal mentors and closest friends. Mel has traveled all over the country working and sharing the stage with industry greats like Jim Rohn, Charlie "Tremendous" Jones, and Bill Bailey just to name a few. With over 31 years experience in both conventional business and network marketing, his wisdom can give you the breakthrough you need to take your success to the next level. Mel also authored a bestselling book, "Questions are the Answers," which gives the reader information and insight about the person who is responsible for 100% of your success...YOU! If I had to describe Mel in one word, I would describe him with the word "Love." He has a wonderful gift to express God's love in the form of caring, sharing, and giving. Mel Brodsky is the mentor who really cares about people.

Hurry! Come with me over here to meet Dr. Jacqueline Sisson, a licensed and ordained minister. What a dynamic women! Business entrepreneur, published author, professional speaker, and marriage therapist, this is one mentor who treats the whole person. An expert in the field of health and nutrition, she can help you gain higher levels of success physically, emotionally, financially, and spiritually. Well versed in the areas of human behavior, she knows the key ingredients on how to help you bring out your full potential, so that you can make everyday the best day of your life.

Now, here we find George Ramirez, witty and hilarious wisdom is the best way to describe George's mentorship. Being close friends and business partners with him for over 15 years, his gift of teaching and his skills as a trainer will help you understand the true components of living a dynamic life. Always fun to be around, he has the uncanny ability to teach you the price of success and, instead of crying about the pain, you laugh your wig off! I remember the first business meeting I had with George. We were scheduled to meet at his luxurious home. I show up in a business suit, and he answers the door in red Bermuda shorts and a sweat band on his head. I said, "I thought we were meeting for business?" He said, "We are! We can talk as we walk." There we were on our first business meeting, power-walking in a million-dollar-home neighborhood—him in tight shorts (it looked to me like they were made out of thin silk) and me in a business suit with wing-tip shoes! I often wondered what people were thinking when they saw us on that eventful day.

Could this be? Yes, I think…yes it is, Gregory Scott Reid "The Millionaire Mentor." What I can say about Gregory is he is true blue in character, honesty, and dedicated to his mission in life, which is to help you reach your goals and dreams. From his bestselling books, "Positive Impact" and "The Millionaire Mentor," and his exciting CD programs, to his exclusive Millionaire Club, he is geared up to help people achieve all they want to be and all they desire to accomplish. From his professional insights to his caring heart, Gregory is a mentor who goes the extra mile. He will make you smile!

What a treat it is to introduce you to Mr. Ruben Gonzales, who is a three-time Olympian and bestselling author. This is a rare opportunity to get insights from a man who knows how to find the Olympian in all of us. Ruben knows first hand the price of winning. The cost of setting a dream, having a vision, staying committed, discipline, and the value of hard work. Most of all, he has a keen understanding of the role mentors play in our lives and in our successes.

Are you getting excited about tapping into the wisdom and insight of all these awesome mentors? I hope you are, because these men and women have cut the pathway for you to reach your golden land of success. Mr. Gregory Scott Reid once said, "Many people get good advice, few profit from it." Because you are reading this book, I know you will be part of the select group that will not only gain wisdom, but will put that wisdom into action.

While we are on the subject of action, this is a perfect time to introduce you to Wil Cason—a man who mastered the art of putting your vision into action. His excellent book, "Visualizing Your Victory," is one of the best books on this subject I have ever read. Many times on the road to success, you will get lost in the forest and lose sight of your destination. Wil Cason is a mentor who helps you get on track, stay on track, and get back on track! Take heed to his message, it has life changing power in it!

A heart of gold—that is how I describe Vincent Gonzales. He has a true Pastor's heart, which means he truly loves people. His gift allows him to reach out to people and not just give good counsel, but allows him to reach people in a non-verbal way to communicate God's love. He is one of the rare mentors who can give us one of the best gifts we could ever ask for—a listening ear (without interrupting every 10 seconds) and a caring heart.

Now coming to the end, I wanted to introduce you to your last mentor—Wanda Mattero, gifted author, trainer, and speaker. Not because she is the last one on the list, but because I wanted to save the best for last. Her gift, her mentorship, is the power of patience. If we could only glean her wisdom on this subject and incorporate it into our lives, how much more enjoyment we would encounter on our journey to success. Success is not based on the law of *instant* but on the law of *growth*. If you open a rose before nature does, you destroy it. If we try to rush success, we destroy that too. Take your time in building your fortune. It will be worth it, and your results will be much better.

Well, there you go. You have met your mentors, now go read, learn, and enjoy each one of their chapters. Oh, by the way, make sure you contact them. They would love to hear from you and hear how they helped you reach your dreams.

Two of the greatest mentors I know,
Mel Brodsky and Charlie "Tremendous" Jones
and me!

Here's to the value of mentors and this extraordinary masterpiece—*The Power of Mentorship*! Without mentors you cannot grow. You cannot succeed. You cannot live a happy, successful, and fulfilled life without mentors, period!!! We are all just shells, our minds are empty, there's nothing there. With this special book you can fill your mind with wisdom and knowledge and learn from the people who have gone before you. Galileo said: "They already know the truth, put some words on it so they can think for themselves of what they already know."

—Charlie "Tremendous" Jones

Chapter 1

The Einstein Factor

Don Boyer

Albert Einstein once said, "I see what everyone sees, but I think what no one else thinks." What set Einstein apart from everyone else and caused him to be one of the most famous physicists of all time? It was his method of thinking—the same principle that separates the rich from the poor.

Everything you have or don't have in your life right now is the direct result of your method of thinking. As long as you hold on to the way you think, you will always get what you currently have. This is not a bad thing if you have everything you want, and you do not desire anything else. However, if you are not happy with the results in your life, the only way to change them is by changing your method of thinking and your belief patterns.

Here are four Einstein Factors to help you change your thinking—to think outside the box or, in other words, to think what only the successful think.

Einstein Factor 1: **"Speak to Your Money"**

Most people have no idea the tremendous power words hold. Words build up and words tear down.

They are contributing factors to both success and failure. Words are not just sounds and syllables, words are containers of energy that affect matter. Words contain elements of power with either positive or negative energy. How you use this energy affects every aspect of your life. The childhood rhyme that says "Sticks and stones may break my bones, but names will never hurt me" is a big fat lie! Bones heal and bruises go away, but cutting words can do damage for a lifetime.

Take some time and do your own personal study of the power and importance of your words. Not only will you find it very enlightening, but it may just be the key that will unleash your hidden potential. It is vital to realize that words contain energy, and money contains energy.

Along with that, understand the law of attraction—like attracts like. That means two masses of matter of the exact same energy and frequencies will move towards each other. Therefore, when you send out words of energy (speaking to your money), they go out there in the universe and attract money like a magnet. This is not based on mumbo-jumbo but exact science and immutable law.

You may be saying to yourself, it can't be that easy, and do you know what? For you, you are right. Doubt breaks the consistency of those two energies, not allowing them to manifest to you. Faith acts as the landing pad and brings that money right to you. Again, this is pure science and laws of quantum physics. You don't have to be an Einstein to use these principles, you just have to put them into practice and believe them.

Write down a sum of money you want to attract in your life. Now, every morning when you get up, begin to verbally call that money to you, and in time, if you do not doubt it, it will come. It is important, when you first start out, to make sure you feel worthy of the amount of money you are calling in.

If you are calling in $10,000 a month, and you have never earned more than $2,000 a month, your inner belief system does not believe you are worth $10,000 a month. Start out with calling in $3,000-$4,000 a month, attain that, and then you move up.

Remember, doubt is not just a product of the head, or what is known as the conscious level of thinking, but mostly the workings of our sub-conscious. It took some of you 20 years or more to get the inner beliefs you now hold, you will not break or change them in 20 minutes. Just keep speaking to your money, and the money will come.

It is the same law that makes the sun rise in the morning and the oceans keep their boundaries. When was the last time you worried about the sun rising? Can't remember when? Well you don't have to worry about the money coming in either. Just remember your words have a dual nature. When you speak words of prosperity and increase, you are at the same time speaking death to lack and poverty. The same holds true on the opposite pole. Every time you speak words of lack and shortage, those same words speak death to abundance and increase. Now go out and "speak to your money."

Einstein Factor 2: **"It's Your Beliefs and Thoughts that Are Holding You Down"**

Just about every student of success and seeker of wealth has read "Think and Grow Rich" by Napoleon Hill. Mr. Hill states that one of the first keys to attaining success is that you must have a burning desire, and that is very true.

The majority of you reading this book have a "burning desire." You know what you want and are even willing to pay the price for it. Yet month after month, and year after year, it seems to elude you. Frustration comes in. You have the discipline, desire, and commitment, you read all the books and go to all the trainings, but you still fall short from reaching your "burning desire"—that level of success you so desperately want.

How can this be? What is the answer? Your burning desire is like a rocket inside of you trying to blast off at full speed, but it is tied down to the launching pad by indestructible chains. You lift off a few inches but are unable to blast off! So, you give it more fuel (trainings, books, CDs, and seminars) hoping to break free and blast off. But you still can't launch. Those chains are unbreakable, but they are not un-lockable.

Those chains consist of your inner belief system that was formed inside of you when you were growing up by well-meaning parents, teachers, friends, and your environment. The fact is we were created for success and engineered for achievement but programmed for failure.

The programming we received during our childhood and adolescent years may not serve us well as adults.

We continue to live by it, because we simply do not know any better...until now.

Another chain is tied to our thoughts, which is formed by our beliefs. No wonder this pursuit of success has been so hard. It's a no-win battle under this kind of arrangement. The problem is not the system, but how we use the system. In fact, this system guarantees success 100% of the time. It will cause you to successfully lose, or successfully win, depending on how you apply it. The key is to get the system working for you. You do this by:

- Being aware of your current beliefs that are holding you back.
- Writing down the things you want and desire.
- Affirming daily that you have your desires.
- Stating daily you are worthy of those desires.
- Speak to those desires, calling them in.

When you practice this and make it part of your lifestyle, you will find yourself reaching your long awaited goals, dreams, and desires. It is not hocus pocus, but the science of your focus.

Einstein Factor 3: **"Success Overnight? I Don't Think So"**

In the quest for success and achievement, please remember this truth. You cannot change your life in one day; however, you can change its direction on any one day that you choose. Success takes time and that is ok, because it allows you to enjoy the journey to the top. Many people equate the climb to success to pain, suffering, and struggle and, in fact, it is the road that most people take. But it's not the only road—or even the best road. Let me show you a better way and for this, once again, we turn to our good friend Albert Einstein and his wonderful understanding of science.

If you drop your pen, what happens? It falls to the ground because of the law of gravity. Unless you are a complete nut, you have never dropped your pen and then stressed out that the law of gravity might not work. Your success and achievement is governed by the same kind of immutable law, so why are you stressing out about it?

Have you heard this—"If you knew you could not fail what would you do?" For many that is just a cliché and holds no reality. Or, as someone once told me, "Yeah, and if my grandmother had hair on her legs, she could be my grandfather." The fact is your success is based on law, and once you understand that and how it works, your success is guaranteed. You can enjoy the ride!

The only reason you struggle so much is you are using the science or laws of success *backwards*. You are attracting problems, shortage, and pain not on purpose but by default. When you are going through hard times and speaking about them, it causes you to constantly think about them, and will only reproduce more of them.

Break the pattern! Change your thinking and your speaking. Hey, what you currently have cannot be changed, but what can be changed is what is in your future. Once a harvest is here (result or conditions), there is no changing it. Even Einstein couldn't change an apple into an orange. But you can plant a different kind of seed and get a different kind of harvest (result or condition).

THINK ABOUT SUCCESS, AND YOU WILL PRODUCE SUCCESS.

THINK ABOUT ABUNDANCE, AND YOU WILL PRODUCE ABUNDANCE.

It won't happen overnight, but it will happen. Just relax and realize your success is guaranteed and go out and enjoy the journey to the top.

Einstein Factor 4: "E + CYS x K = DR"

EMOTION "Energy in Motion" stands for the first letter in our equation. Emotion is a very powerful force; in fact one of the most powerful forces on the planet. It has the ability to unleash the scientific genius inside of man, allowing us to travel into space and back, but also has the ability to unleash the torrents of hell and bring upon mankind the vilest kind of destruction.

When you are first in love with someone, you turn into a Superman or Superwomen who can go days without food or sleep, and endowed with endless energy and wit. The age factor has nothing to do with it when this force is in full bloom. It is the power of energy in motion in the direction of love.

What you want to do is get that "energy in motion" aimed at your goals and dreams. Once you get excited, motivated, and turned-on about your dreams, that energy will propel you like a rocket towards them. But a word of caution must be stated here. That energy or emotion that is traveling towards your dreams can be redirected to travel away from them by people and circumstances. Here you are all excited about your goals and dreams and fired up, and you go and share them with someone who has done nothing other than live life like the backend of a horse dropping road apples on the ground, who tells you, "You can't do that!".

Young Joseph in the Bible could relate. When he told his dreams to his brothers, they threw him in a pit and sold him as a slave!

Listen, when people tell you what cannot be done, they are exposing *their* limitations, not yours. Don't allow people to steal your dreams by redirecting your energy in motion (emotions) away from them. Your success will never be celebrated among the average, only in the encampment of winners. This is why Mentors are so important to our success. Our Mentors cheer us on and become the voice of reasoning that says, "Yes, you CAN do it!"

The first ingredient to our success equation is emotion, so get excited about your dreams. The next time someone tells you that you won't reach your dreams, look them right in the eye and say "Your Cool-low is out of here!" (Cool-low is rear end in Spanish...I think).

CYS stands for being **COMMITTED to YOUR SUCCESS**. Right now you have mentors, family members, and friends committed to your success. The only one left to be committed is you. You have to be committed to your own success. When you are committed to your success, it gives you the driving and staying power to overcome obstacles, temptations, and distractions. When you want to give up, your commitment says, "No!" and you keep on going. Unless you are committed to your own success,

26

it really does not matter who else is committed or behind you. Other people cannot help you if you are not 100% dedicated to your cause.

If you do a careful study of the ancient and Holy Scriptures, you will find that God tells us to "Decree a thing, and I will establish it," and in the book of Proverbs He says, "I create the fruit of the lips." In other words, He gives us the scientific equation of the law of attraction. In layman terms, God said to name it (your success or desires) and claim it. What most do is name it failure and blame it—I can't be successful because of my spouse, or I can't become rich because of…. The list could fill 5,000 books. When you are committed to your own success, you will have no time to play the blame game. You will be out there carving out your own good fortune and enjoying life.

The letter K stands for **KNOWLEDGE**. The day you stop learning is the day you stop growing. And when you stop growing that is the day you stop living. Oh you may still have breath in your lungs, and walk around, but as someone said, "Many die at 40 and don't get buried until they're 70."

Knowledge is the fuel that takes your dreams from your heart and transforms them into your hand. I ask people, "Will you dream of achievement or will you achieve your dreams?" Most everyone has some kind of dream to be more, have more, and do more. Yet the sad fact is 97% of all those people will never experience their dreams.

The only thing that keeps people from their dreams is knowledge. Some might say, action is the most important part, however, if you have the right kind of knowledge, it will cause you to take action.

I was talking with the legendary William E. Bailey (a man who had a personal meeting with the Pope, lunch with Neil Armstrong 6 months after he returned from the moon, and created a business that produced $64 million dollars per month in its prime) and asked him, "Why do so many fail to climb the millionaire mountain?" After a long discussion, he said one of the primary reasons was a lack of knowledge. Knowledge comes in many forms, much you learn by reading and study, but some comes only from the care and wisdom of a mentor. Mentors do hold the golden key to unleash your potential and unlock your future.

DR stands for **DESIRED RESULTS**, the last letters of the Einstein Equation. As our good friend and mentor, Albert Einstein, would agree, if you go into your success lab and take the ingredients of positive **emotion** and being **committed to your success**, mix it with **knowledge**, you will get your **desired results**.

Don Boyer is an outstanding public speaker and published author. He resides in Southern California and can be contacted at donboyer@realifeteaching.com or by calling (562) 237-8039.

Chapter 2

The Ultimate Goal Setting System

Carmelo S. Flores

Goals Are Dreams with a Deadline

Have you ever felt lost or confused? Have you ever wondered if you would ever arrive? Have you ever thought that there must be a more efficient way to set and achieve goals? If you answered yes to at least one of these questions, you will be glad you have come across "The Ultimate Goal Setting System!"

For many years, I too ran around like a chicken without a head, like a dog chasing its tail, and I still did not achieve the results I was searching for when setting goals. I began taking courses on goal setting. I attended the workshops, read the books, and listened to the cassettes.

Yes, I went to "the seminar!" I discovered that most of what I heard was the same stuff and, in many cases, it was impractical or unrealistic. Some of those workshops were very confusing, not to mention very expensive. It is because of those reasons that I was inspired to come up with something practical, something reasonable, and within the reach of everyone.

I have held for many years the belief that if a sixth grader can understand something, so can a doctor or lawyer. That is why I have kept the system basic and simple.

After all, fundamentals are basic and old. It is from these old fundamentals that I have developed what I believe to be the most basic, simple, and yet the most effective goal setting system anywhere—The Ultimate Goal Setting System.

I invite you to a new journey to your future. Remember—no pressure, no diamond!

THE SEVEN GAUGES

1. FAITH (spiritual)
2. FAMILY (immediate and extended)
3. FRIENDS (society)
4. BODY (physical)
5. MIND (emotions)
6. CAREER (contributions)
7. MONEY (financial)

The seven gauges represent the seven major areas of our lives. If we think of any problem or challenge, any dream or desire we can imagine, it will fit within one of the seven gauges. In the following pages, you will see that goal setting really is like a puzzle. We will put the pieces together one by one.

First, we will begin by talking about and explaining the dashboard of my life—or your life. Then, we will talk about the windshield on the dashboard and what you may see in front of you. I will then explain the seven gauges one by one in more detail, and you will see how it all starts falling into place and making sense.

We will continue by doing a few more exercises about where you are and where you want to go, followed by steps you must apply to arrive. Finally, after careful planning and doing, we will review your results.

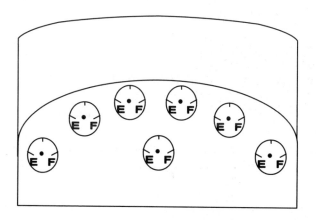

THE DASHBOARD OF MY LIFE

I chose a dashboard to explain the Ultimate Goal Setting System because most of us are used to looking at one daily while we drive our cars. We keep a close eye on the gauges which gives us an indication about the vehicle's performance and overall condition. Many years ago, I asked myself "what if I had a dashboard with gauges in my life that I could look at on a regular basis to check and evaluate my performance and overall condition?" The idea was born and with it, The Ultimate Goal Setting System!

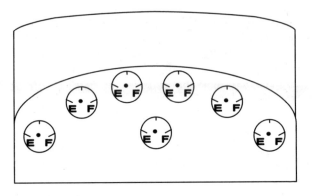

EXERCISE 1

Draw the road you see ahead of you today.

In this exercise, draw inside the windshield (above), the road you see ahead of you. Make believe that your eyes are the windshield. What does the road look like ahead of you? Draw it in detail along with its surroundings.

Your drawing is representative of where you feel you are now both socially and emotionally, e.g., do you feel pressured in a busy grid lock on a freeway or do you feel lonely on a dark desert highway?

Faith is the core belief we hold about God, ourselves and others and the world around us. Most of us express our faith in a religious or spiritual way.

Our families are the only people whom we do not choose. Immediate or extended, obviously someone thought them to be the most important people on earth to us.

Friends are the people in society we choose to share our most precious commodity with—our time! A true friend is like a soft pillow where we rest our heads after the struggles of dealing with our families. Smile, laugh, or cry, a true friend is always there near by.

Our body is like a temple entrusted to us while we live. It is our duty to see to it that our body serves us healthy, strong, and graciously for the course of our journey in life.

We decide how we feel with our mind! It is unique and sacred. No other living, breathing creature may enter it without our permission. If your mind can conceive and your heart can believe, you will achieve!

Our career is how we choose to contribute and serve our communities and society. The key is to choose a career that allows us to feel fulfilled while allowing us to walk tall and proud.

Money is the gift we receive for taking good care of the other six areas of our lives. It appears that the better job we do with the other six areas, the greater the reward we receive.

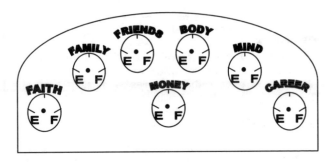

EXERCISE 2

Observe the seven gauges on the dashboard in front of you. Look at them individually and note that each one has an E indicating Empty and an F indicating Full. Evaluate these seven gauges and draw a needle inside each one representative of whether you feel empty, full, or somewhere in between in that area of your life.

EXERCISE 3

On a scale of 1-7: Where am I now?

1. FAITH (spiritual)   ____
2. FAMILY (immediate and extended)   ____
3. FRIENDS (society)   ____
4. BODY (physical)   ____
5. MIND (emotions)   ____
6. CAREER (contributions)   ____
7. MONEY (financial)   ____

EXERCISE:
Evaluate where you feel you are today in every major area of your life on a scale of one to seven. One is the lowest or weakest and seven is the highest or strongest.

EXERCISE 4

On a scale of 1-7, where do I want to be in 1 hour, 1 day, 1 week, 1 month, 2 months, or 3 months?

(CIRCLE ONE)

1. FAITH (spiritual):

1 hour	1	2	3	4	5	6	7
1 day	1	2	3	4	5	6	7
1 week	1	2	3	4	5	6	7
1 month	1	2	3	4	5	6	7
2 months	1	2	3	4	5	6	7
3 months	1	2	3	4	5	6	7

2. FAMILY (immediate and extended):

1 hour	1	2	3	4	5	6	7
1 day	1	2	3	4	5	6	7
1 week	1	2	3	4	5	6	7
1 month	1	2	3	4	5	6	7
2 months	1	2	3	4	5	6	7
3 months	1	2	3	4	5	6	7

3. FRIENDS (society):

1 hour	1	2	3	4	5	6	7
1 day	1	2	3	4	5	6	7
1 week	1	2	3	4	5	6	7
1 month	1	2	3	4	5	6	7
2 months	1	2	3	4	5	6	7
3 months	1	2	3	4	5	6	7

4. BODY (physical):

1 hour	1	2	3	4	5	6	7
1 day	1	2	3	4	5	6	7
1 week	1	2	3	4	5	6	7
1 month	1	2	3	4	5	6	7
2 months	1	2	3	4	5	6	7
3 months	1	2	3	4	5	6	7

5. MIND (emotions):

1 hour	1	2	3	4	5	6	7
1 day	1	2	3	4	5	6	7
1 week	1	2	3	4	5	6	7
1 month	1	2	3	4	5	6	7
2 months	1	2	3	4	5	6	7
3 months	1	2	3	4	5	6	7

6. CAREER (contributions):

1 hour	1	2	3	4	5	6	7
1 day	1	2	3	4	5	6	7
1 week	1	2	3	4	5	6	7
1 month	1	2	3	4	5	6	7
2 months	1	2	3	4	5	6	7
3 months	1	2	3	4	5	6	7

7. MONEY (financial):

1 hour	1	2	3	4	5	6	7
1 day	1	2	3	4	5	6	7
1 week	1	2	3	4	5	6	7
1 month	1	2	3	4	5	6	7
2 months	1	2	3	4	5	6	7
3 months	1	2	3	4	5	6	7

EXERCISE:

Decide whether you wish, or need, to set a one-hour goal in a crisis or emergency situation, a long-term goal that is three months away or something in the middle. Then set a realistic goal about where you want to arrive during that period of time in relation to where you are today.

EXERCISE 5

7 Steps to Reach Your Goal:

1. Write down the date and time you wish to achieve it.

2. Write down the obstacles you will need to face and overcome.

3. Identify the knowledge and skills you will need to get there.

4. Write down clearly and specifically what you wish to accomplish.

5. List the names of the people and groups with whom you will work.

6. Develop your plan of action and write it down.

7. Ask—Why am I doing this? What's in it for me?

EXERCISE:

Apply each of these seven steps to every major area of your life in the following pages beginning with your faith and concluding with money.

FAITH

The most important belief I hold about my faith is—

Follow through by using these seven steps:

1. A clear and specific vision of my goal is:

2. The date and time by which I will reach my goal is:

3. The obstacles I will need to face and overcome are:

4. The knowledge and skills I will need to get there are:

5. The people and groups I will work with are:

6. My plan of action to reach this goal is:

7. The reason why I am doing this is:

FAMILY

The most important belief I hold about my family is—

Follow through by using these seven steps:

1. A clear and specific vision of my goal is:

2. The date and time by which I will reach my goal is:

3. The obstacles I will need to face and overcome are:

4. The knowledge and skills I will need to get there are:

5. The people and groups I will work with are:

6. My plan of action to reach this goal is:

7. The reason why I am doing this is:

FRIENDS

The most important belief I hold about my friends is—

Follow through by using these seven steps:

1. A clear and specific vision of my goal is:

2. The date and time by which I will reach my goal is:

3. The obstacles I will need to face and overcome are:

4. The knowledge and skills I will need to get there are:

5. The people and groups I will work with are:

6. My plan of action to reach this goal is:

7. The reason why I am doing this is:

BODY

The most important belief I hold about my body is—

Follow through by using these seven steps:

1. A clear and specific vision of my goal is:

2. The date and time by which I will reach my goal is:

3. The obstacles I will need to face and overcome are:

4. The knowledge and skills I will need to get there are:

5. The people and groups I will work with are:

6. My plan of action to reach this goal is:

7. The reason why I am doing this is:

MIND

The most important belief I hold about my mind is—

Follow through by using these seven steps:

1. A clear and specific vision of my goal is:

2. The date and time by which I will reach my goal is:

3. The obstacles I will need to face and overcome are:

4. The knowledge and skills I will need to get there are:

5. The people and groups I will work with are:

6. My plan of action to reach this goal is:

7. The reason why I am doing this is:

CAREER

The most important belief I hold about my career is—

Follow through by using these seven steps:

1. A clear and specific vision of my goal is:

2. The date and time by which I will reach my goal is:

3. The obstacles I will need to face and overcome are:

4. The knowledge and skills I will need to get there are:

5. The people and groups I will work with are:

6. My plan of action to reach this goal is:

7. The reason why I am doing this is:

MONEY

The most important belief I hold about money is—

Follow through by using these seven steps:

1. A clear and specific vision of my goal is:

2. The date and time by which I will reach my goal is:

3. The obstacles I will need to face and overcome are:

4. The knowledge and skills I will need to get there are:

5. The people and groups I will work with are:

6. My plan of action to reach this goal is:

7. The reason why I am doing this is:

EXERCISE 6

The time has now come to take action. In this exercise you will carry out all of the plans that you have written in the prior exercises.

**OUR DESTINY IS SHAPED
IN A SIMPLE MOMENT OF DECISION...**

DECIDE TO DO IT AND DO IT NOW!!!

DO OR DO NOT! THERE IS NO TRY!

EXERCISE 7

In exercises 1 through 5 you set your goals and developed your plans of action. In exercise 6 you followed through and took action. Now in exercise 7 it's time to review your results.

REVIEW:

A) Are you satisfied with your results? If you are, congratulations!!! It's time to celebrate! If you are not, find out what is missing!

B) Are you ready to move on to your next level? If you are, go to Exercise 1 and continue the journey. If you are not, find out why—what's holding you back?

C) What can you do differently the next time? If you are satisfied with your results, aim higher and stick with what works! If you are not satisfied with your results, ask yourself:

"Why not?"
"What else can I read?"
"Who else can I ask for counsel and support?"

The ULTIMATE Goal-Setting System

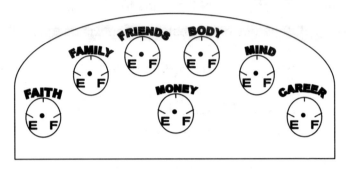

7 GAUGES TO EVALUATE

On a scale of 1-7, where am I now?
(1 = the lowest, 7 = the highest)

1.	FAITH (spiritual)	1 2 3 4 5 6 7
2.	FAMILY (immediate and extended)	1 2 3 4 5 6 7
3.	FRIENDS (society)	1 2 3 4 5 6 7
4.	BODY (physical)	1 2 3 4 5 6 7
5.	MIND (emotions)	1 2 3 4 5 6 7
6.	CAREER (contributions)	1 2 3 4 5 6 7
7.	MONEY (financial)	1 2 3 4 5 6 7

On a scale of 1-7, where do I want to be?
(1 = the lowest, 7 = the highest)

1.	FAITH (spiritual)	1 2 3 4 5 6 7
2.	FAMILY (immediate and extended)	1 2 3 4 5 6 7
3.	FRIENDS (society)	1 2 3 4 5 6 7
4.	BODY (physical)	1 2 3 4 5 6 7
5.	MIND (emotions)	1 2 3 4 5 6 7
6.	CAREER (contributions)	1 2 3 4 5 6 7
7.	MONEY (financial)	1 2 3 4 5 6 7

7 STEPS TO REACH THESE GOALS

1. Write down the date and time you wish to achieve it.
2. Write down the obstacles you will need to face and overcome.
3. Identify the knowledge and skills you will need to get there.
4. Write down clearly and specifically what you wish to accomplish.
5. List the names of the people and groups with whom you will work.
6. Develop your plan of action and write it down.
7. Ask—Why am I doing this? What's in it for me?

OUR DESTINY IS SHAPED
IN A SIMPLE MOMENT OF DECISION

DECIDE TO DO IT AND DO IT NOW!!!

The most important belief I hold about _____ is:

Follow through by using these seven steps:

1. A clear and specific vision of my goal is:
2. The date and time by which I will reach my goal is:
3. The obstacles I will need to face and overcome:
4. The knowledge and skills I will need to get there:
5. The people and groups I will work with are:
6. My plan of action to reach this goal is:
7. The reason why I am doing this is:

Carmelo Flores is an extraordinary businessman, speaker, trainer, and a top leader in his company. Contact him at:
(951) 786-7479
platino@prepaidlegal.com
www.prepaidlegal.com/hub/platino

Chapter 3

The Five Most Important Things I Learned From My Mentor Jim Rohn

Jerry Haines

Over 30 years ago, I attended a seminar in San Jose, California, that changed my life. The seminar was being conducted by a unique man—Jim Rohn. At first, I really didn't want to be there. A good friend had suggested I go and hear this remarkable man. She said he had a message about life strategies that would be beneficial for me to hear.

At that time, I wasn't interested in attending any kind of seminar. I didn't need to hear about any life strategies, even though I wasn't doing well personally or financially. I was one of those "know it alls." I was more interested in watching TV. I averaged about 6-7 hours per day of television watching. My favorite programs were *The Six Million Dollar Man*, *Wonder Woman*, and *The Bionic Woman*, just to name a few.

Although I wasn't interested in attending, my friend still bought a seminar ticket for me and convinced me to go at the last moment. She said, "It won't hurt to at least check it out. Besides, I already bought you a ticket." Reluctantly, I went to the seminar. I missed one of my favorite programs too—*The Bionic Woman, Part II.*

When we got to the seminar room, it was packed with hundreds of people. It looked like there were no seats left. The usher at the door told us there were two seats left. Guess where they were? In front of the stage and that's where we sat. I felt stuck. I wanted to sit in the back so I could leave early.

As we waited for the seminar to begin, we could feel the energy in the room, and hear the excitement, in anticipation of what was about to happen. I was asked by my friend if I wanted paper to take notes. Thinking there would be no reason to write anything down, I declined. What could I possibly hear here that would be important enough to me to want to have it on paper?

They introduced the speaker, Jim Rohn. This silver-haired, sophisticated-looking gentleman walked onto the stage. He had the look of confidence in his demeanor. I was skeptical, but I said to myself, *Jim Rohn give me your best shot!*

For the first 30 minutes, I listened closely. The more I listened, the more I realized he had a message I needed. The message was vital to me. I borrowed paper from my friend and started taking notes.

This wise man spoke the plain truth. It was hard to disagree with him. He said, "Life change begins with the truth, and you cannot change what you do not ever acknowledge." He was certainly sharing some golden nuggets for success in life. His inspirational message provoked me to do some much-needed self-examination of my present life.

I walked out of that seminar with 14 pages of notes. That seminar changed my life! It was the night that turned my life around. I left disgusted by the results I had, up until then, in my personal and financial life. I made a decision to change my life—that night. I am not the same person I was then, over 30 years ago.

There was an opening for a sales rep in San Jose at a company called Adventures in Achievement, to promote Mr. Rohn's seminar. I decided to be part of the company, because I felt everyone could benefit from hearing Jim's message. I wanted to reach as many people as possible, and this was the best way to do that.

For the next 30 years, until I retired in June 2005, I was associated with Jim Rohn. In those 30 years, I spoke to over 11,000 companies, with over 1 million people in attendance, sharing Jim's philosophies. I was able to successfully bring over 200 public seminars by Mr. Rohn to many cities throughout the United States. I am truly grateful to have been associated with this unique gentleman of great wisdom who taught me so much about life and how it works best.

From countless taxi rides, plane flights, dinners, phone calls, and private conversations, here are the 5 most important things I learned from my mentor and close friend. They have helped me become successful in promoting his seminars, ideas, and philosophies, and make big improvements in my personal life.

A Game Plan for Life

First, Jim taught me, and many of us, that life is to be treated seriously. Life is not a joke. This is not a practice session—it's the real deal. Many of us go through life treating it casually. Jim says in his seminars, "Don't be casual about your life, because casualness leads to casualties."

Thirty years ago, I was not that serious about anything in my life, and I had plenty of casualties. He suggested to me to put together a game plan. He called it a game plan for living your life on purpose and with a purpose. He said the best way to become more serious and eliminate the casualties was to have a detailed plan of action that would create a balanced life.

He talked about designing the next 10 years on paper. That sounded difficult. I wasn't even sure what I was doing the next day. But I wanted so badly to make the changes from just getting by to achieving much more in my life. I decided right after that seminar to sit down and design my future on paper.

It took me 2 weeks to finally have it completed. It was plain hard work. That's why a lot of people don't do it. But as I always heard from my teacher, you've got to be willing to pay the price and make the effort to have anything worthwhile in your life.

I learned over the years from Jim the many reasons why it is necessary to have an activity plan. Let me give you some of those reasons it made sense to me.

First, without a well-defined plan for the many important areas of our lives, there is a chance we will make poor choices. Before I heard Mr. Rohn's program, I found myself waking up each morning being uncertain, unsure, and hesitant about my life and direction. Consequently, I made many poor choices. Design a daily, monthly, and yearly detailed plan of action. You will wake up every day feeling more certain, more deliberate, and more inspired by what you see coming, and it'll show up in a more confident way in everything you do each day.

Second, it is easy to get off track. We all have temptations, distractions, and obstacles that get in the way of us succeeding in our lives and businesses. A daily activity plan will keep us focused and steady. I found, when I was promoting Jim's program, the best way to stay on track was to have a tight schedule set up for everything I needed to do every day.

What worked best for me was to have an impending event, like a seminar. That put the pressure on me to stick with my plan every day and let nothing interfere. I was called a human machine. Every day leading up to the date of the seminar, I would have meetings to speak to groups about the program. I would do some prospecting, then go home and make some phone calls to get referrals, do follow-ups, and set up more meetings. I did this religiously every day. I made sure that nothing got in the way. If one of my friends called me just to talk, I would tell them it wasn't a good time.

One of the reasons I was driven to be so focused was I never wanted Jim speaking in front of a *half-full* room. I made sure that the seminars had anywhere from 1,300 to 2,000 people every time, because Jim used to say, "I don't do well in an empty room." We made quite a team. He was good at what he did best (speak), and I was good at what I did best (promote).

Third, the reason to have a game plan is because it's better to operate from *making* it happen rather than *wishing* it would happen. Too many people cross their fingers and hope that the day will turn out okay. That is not a good plan. This game plan is a commitment plan, activity plan, a get-going plan, and a plan that gets you excited, inspired, and passionate about your future—an I-can't-wait-to-get-to-the-day kind of plan.

Living life with passion is the key, and that's a challenge for many people. I understood that when I spoke to the many companies on Jim's ideas. I saw people who had no passion in these meetings and, consequently, their sales numbers were not that good. I remember reading this line in the book, *Success at Life,* by the founders of Republic Tea—"Years wrinkle the skin, but to live without passion wrinkles the soul."

I certainly saw a lot of wrinkled souls in my years with Rohn. So make sure you have a well-thought-out daily activity plan for your spiritual life, relationships, finances, association with the right people, personal development, and health—a plan that creates for you a passion and a desire to live your life with intensity.

Finally, what Jim constantly taught me was that the promise of the future, well-designed, was an awesome force. Question: Are you in awe of your future? Do you like what you see coming? If not, you can fix where you are headed right now by taking Jim's advice and creating a powerful game plan that has you fired up.

Personal Development—Getting Better
The key to building a good life is working harder on yourself than you do on anything else. It's called personal development. The process of getting better

and growing is not easy. In fact, it's plain hard work, as most of you would agree. But we must grow if we want to bring more value to the marketplace to receive better pay. Jim says your income seldom exceeds your personal growth.

In the beginning, when I first started out promoting Jim's seminars, I lacked a lot of necessary skills to be successful. One of the skills I lacked was the ability to communicate effectively in front of groups. It was one of my biggest fears. I remember in college receiving a D in my speech class. So, in those early talks that I gave, I was not very good. My face turned all kinds of colors of fear, and I would forget my lines. Oh, it was bad! However, I became the top sales person in San Jose month after month. It was not through skill, so it must have been through determination.

People bought tickets to see Jim's seminar, because they saw my sincerity and honesty. I became better because I worked on myself really hard. I read books on public speaking, I listened to other speakers, and I went to classes.

One day back in February 1976, I stopped by the corporate office to drop off some paperwork around lunch hour and the only person in the office was Jim. I knocked on the door and said, "Can I ask you a question?" He said, "Sure please have a seat."

I took the opportunity and admitted, "I can't seem to get comfortable speaking in front of these different groups. Do you have any suggestions?"

He asked me if I had seen a good movie lately. I said, "Yes, I have." He questioned me, "Did you tell a friend about the movie?" I answered, "Yes, I did." He said, "That's the same approach you would have speaking in front of groups of people. Talk to each group as if they were friends of yours and just tell them the experience you had attending the seminar and what you got out of it. Maybe the message will benefit them as it did you."

I took that advice and my sales skyrocketed. I felt much more relaxed in front of groups. I really worked on my speaking. As the years passed, I found myself becoming more confident, and I noticed my income growing every year because I was getting better.

Eventually, the rest of the skills I worked on, such as time management, leadership, and sales, helped me to start earning a good six-figure income. Now I have piles of possessions, but that's not important. What's important is what I became from all my hard work.

After you strip away all the materialistic things you have, who are you really? I truly believe, as Mr. Rohn taught, to never sell out. Do the right thing no matter what, and make sure you stick with good morals and values. I also learned over the years to chisel my character; and one of the areas I feel is most important is being and staying humble. Never let your ego get in the way.

For me, Jim is a good example of someone who doesn't let his ego get in the way. He is truly a humble man. This is all part of getting better. The key is always being a work in progress and never thinking you have arrived.

But all that I just talked about requires discipline. Jim taught me about the power of discipline and how engaging in a few simple disciplines, practiced each day, will affect my life in a positive way. And let me say, true discipline is not easy. There is no Easy Street. Easy Street is a dead end street.

In the book by Scott Peck, *The Road Less Traveled*, there is the line—"Life is difficult." And it is. Life isn't easy for any of us. I just lost my Dad suddenly. I'm still dealing with the emptiness. It hasn't been easy on my Mom. She was married to Dad for 59½ years. We all have things we are dealing with that make life difficult.

There is a classic line you might have heard, "Life is simple but not easy." The best way to make your life much easier and deal with the challenges we all face is to engage in daily disciplines. Here are some of the daily disciplines I have engaged in that have helped me become a better person and live a much fuller life.

I worked on my philosophy. Jim stated 30 years ago the biggest determining factor of how well my life works out was how I thought. The best way to see how I was thinking was to simply look at my bottom line numbers. Sales numbers, bank account numbers, investment numbers, health numbers, spiritual hours, and family hours, all tell the story of how well I was thinking. He said the numbers don't lie.

My numbers were not looking good. Of course back then I wasn't thinking too clearly. It is so true that your present bank balance is a clear indication of your present philosophy of life. And if you don't like the numbers, change your philosophy.

He said, "Build a strong personal philosophy that's going to guide you through the good times and the bad times." The lesson I learned was that the battle is always on. Never ever let your guard down. The best way not to let your guard down and be mentally tough is to discipline yourself to constantly fine tune your thinking, by seeking out ideas from several different sources. What's good to remember here is that life is a matter of odds. If you want the odds in your favor, you discipline yourself to bring in the wisdom.

I like to read at least one hour per day on different subjects. My mentor taught me to be a student—a student in my business, a student father, a student husband, etc. Do the mental sweat to gather up ideas from reading, listening to CDs, watching DVDs, attending seminars, going to classes; and all the things that fine tune our thinking, so we make better decisions to increase the odds of having better health, better relationships, and better financial numbers.

Are you reading the books, attending the classes, and going to the seminars that are going to take you where you wish to be in the next 5 years? I remember Jim saying to an audience in South Africa, "If you think you have all the answers, you might want to start asking some different questions."

A suggestion for a discipline on how to develop better thinking habits is to associate with the right people. Get around people who are going places, people who are growing, and people who are excited about their life. I associate with people who inspire me to get to the next level. I'm around people who talk about how to build a better life. It's always good to get around a mastermind group and knock around some good ideas to build a more successful business.

Don't hang out with negative people or the complainers. My mentor used to say many years ago, "Even by accident your so-called close friends could put strychnine in your coffee, so watch your coffee!"

Beware of where you receive your input. Most people would rather be negative than positive. Over the last 30 years, I have read a lot of books, and I haven't found any books on "The Power of Negative Thinking." I did find a book, "The Power of Positive Thinking," however, and I hope you have had a chance to read this great book by Norman Vincent Peale.

Building a Healthy Attitude
The third most important thing I learned from my mentor was how you feel makes a big difference in how well you will do in life. If you don't feel well emotionally you won't do well. Attitude really is everything. How you feel when you wake up everyday to face the world is so important.

Over the years, I have met thousands of sales people throughout this country and what I observed the most was that a large percentage had poor attitudes. The reason most of them had poor attitudes was because their sales numbers and their income numbers were not that good. The majority of the sales managers wanted me to speak to their sales teams about developing better attitudes. Other sales managers thought their people needed more sales training. In my opinion, sales training and sales skills are important, but that won't get you out of bed on a Monday morning all excited. I teach them what Jim has taught me, which is what's going to get you out of bed everyday excited and inspired. It's called having a big "why to."

The reason most people don't do well in sales is because they are mostly affected by poor past results. They are especially in trouble if their numbers aren't looking good. I was always taught to borrow from the past for the experience and borrow from the future for today's inspiration. Be mostly affected by what you see coming and let that inspire you every day. To be blunt, like my teacher, smart people without reasons usually don't succeed in the business world. They are bright and broke. They are the ones who are not that ambitious or inspired. Their "why-to" isn't that big.

When I first started with AIA, the training was excellent, but that wasn't what motivated me to succeed in the business. What motivated me was my list of reasons why I wanted to do well. I had financial reasons, family reasons, benevolent reasons, personal development reasons, and the sense of accomplishment. I had my "why-to" list so well defined, I was able to get through the most difficult days, which included disappointments and rejection.

Finally, something to always remember—reasons come first and answers come second. With reasons, you are driven to go find the answers. When you have plenty of reasons, you are eager to go look for the books, attend the classes, and do the exercises.

Jim was right. After I put together my list of reasons; I woke up everyday with a healthy, positive attitude. I felt really good about my future, and I started to receive good results in my life. When you have a good healthy, positive attitude, you certainly do see things a lot differently.

Activity—Plugging in Full Effort

The fourth and most important lesson I learned was, after putting a plan together, seek out wisdom and find ways to feel good about the future. Now it was time to actually go to work. Now that I had the formula for success, it was time to plug in full effort.

In order for us to have the success we want, we must take all that we are (from the skills we have developed) to the marketplace and put them to work. Instead of dreaming about the promise of the future, we must actually do something about it. Jim always taught me that talking about achievement is one thing; making it happen is something altogether different.

After I put a game plan together with all my hopes and dreams, I got excited. I started telling people about all my dreams, about how much money I was going to be making, the big house I was going to be living in, and the expensive car I was going to be driving. I started living in delusion and then it dawned on me one day that for all this to happen and to back up my talk, I needed to do some actual labor. I didn't want to fall in to the "someday" thinking and wishing I should have and could have done something more with my life.

So, I decided to commit to having a consistent disciplined activity that would ensure me good results. I noticed when I actually went to work putting in full effort (massive action), I became one of the top producers in promoting Jim's public seminars. Not only that, my self-confidence started to soar. This inspired me to do even more, become even better.

Going half effort in anything wasn't for me anymore. Most people I have met over the years are into just getting by, doing just enough. I believe one of the most important messages of Jim's seminars is when he talks about the two personal pains that no one escapes. One is the pain of discipline; the other is the pain of regret. One weighs ounces and the other weighs tons—or one will cost you pennies, the other a fortune. That pain of regret is tough which comes from neglect. Neglecting the daily disciplines could cost you. You can face the pain of discipline today, or you can avoid the pain of discipline and face the disaster down the road called the big balloon payment.

Being broke doesn't happen overnight; usually the wrong pain was picked. Your health doesn't usually disappear overnight. Probably the wrong pain was picked. That's why I'm on my diet and exercise program. Marriages usually don't disappear overnight. Not paying attention might be the cause. Having a bad sales month doesn't happen overnight. Usually it's from not engaging in the daily activity that results in having poor numbers. The pain of regret really does weigh tons. You can see some people bent over from the weight.

Question: What pain have you picked so far this month, this year? The answer is your bottom line numbers: Sales numbers, income numbers, investment numbers, health numbers, spiritual hours, family hours, and the number of books you have read. The numbers don't lie. You are either on track or off track.

Reality is always the best beginning. When we accept the truth, then we'll probably start making the changes. The change I made was to start doing a few simple disciplines every day that was creating for me a more balanced life.

Take Time to Reflect

The fifth and I feel most rewarding thing I learned from my friend and teacher was to take the time and do some self-examination. Take time out often for you. I really enjoy the time I spend with my wife, Barbara, but I also really enjoy taking time out for me. On weekends, I like to go to the Saguaro National Park in Tucson where we live, and find a quiet place where I park and sit and think about my life. I reflect on what happened the last week—the people I met, the calls I made, the experiences I had. It's a time to pause, reflect and take a look at where I am headed, and make some corrections so my next week will be better in all areas over the last week. Jim calls it gathering up the past week and investing it into the next week.

Jim talked about keeping a journal. He said if your life is worth living it's worth recording. Ever since he sold me on that idea I have been keeping a journal of my daily life experiences. On my weekends or whenever I take the time to reflect, I go back over what I wrote in my journal. I have learned so much about myself just by remembering about how I felt about some things because I wrote them down and didn't trust my memory. By breaking away and pausing to reflect and doing some self-examination, it has been helpful for me to make some on-course corrections. Also during this time of reflection, I write down all that I am grateful for. I make a list in my journal so I never forget. I'm grateful for my wife, Barbara, who has made my life complete and has given me strong support. I'm grateful for my many loyal friends who have inspired me over the years. I am thankful for so many things. I especially want to thank, Jim Rohn, my mentor and friend for teaching me so many valuable lessons. I also want to thank him for his loyalty and friendship all these years.

Remember, you have a very precious life, so make it a great day everyday.

Jerry Haines has devoted his life to the study of the fundamentals of human behavior. Based on his 30 year association with Jim Rohn, he has made a career of understanding personal motivation and how it affects performance. Jerry is recognized as a talented speaker and effective trainer. He has spoken to over 11,000 companies covering topics like: Winning Through the Refinement of Philosophy, The Importance of Discipline in Our Life, and The Five Most Important Lessons to Learn and Developing a Game Plan for Living Life on Purpose. You can contact Jerry at 800-553-0840 or email: glhent@earthlink.net.

www.strivingforgreatness.com

Chapter 4

Destined for Purpose

David Diaz

Destiny: the seeming inevitable course of events.

Destine: to be determined or seem to be determined for a special goal or purpose.

Destination: the place to which someone or something is going or being sent.

Have you ever wondered about the direction of your life? Well stop wondering and start knowing. Destiny is not complicated or farfetched. Destiny is actually a word associated with the word destination. In other words, I believe there is a destined place in life where all of us want to arrive; whether it's to be a millionaire, have a better marriage, or start your own business.

Purpose is having a predetermined idea that gives us a reason why we do what we do, and it gives reason for passion to exist. If an architect doesn't have blueprints that give him purpose of how to build, then he will build with confusion and bewilderment. I've seen many people, young and old, without any purpose in life—living from one day to the next. Before departing on a trip, isn't there a place you have in mind before you arrive? What about your life?

I'm reminded of a scripture in the Bible of where God is speaking to His people and He says, "My people are destroyed for lack of knowledge." Imagine God's very own people can reserve the right to be destroyed for a lack of knowledge or know-how. If a *lack of knowledge* can lead to destruction, imagine what having knowledge can bring. It can bring the opposite of destruction and that is life, wholeness, and prosperity.

As you read this chapter, read it slow and meditate on it. It will bring tailored revelation to fit in your own life that will bring to life new ideas and concepts. It will resurrect old dreams and goals that will cause you to reach your destination in life.

Number One on the Road to Your Destination is VISION

From Martin Luther King to Christopher Columbus, there have been many great men and women that have walked the stage of life. They have lived and gone on but what remains is their vision fulfilled.

Vision is the ability to see the end from the beginning. It gives reality to our future and, in most cases, the vision may be contrary to your past and present. In Habakkuk 2:2, "Record the vision and inscribe it on tablets that the one who reads it may run." The vision helps us to run with a focus in mind.

Many people are running in life with no vision, and according to God's standards, we should run with a vision. I call running with a vision progress, and I call running without a vision, just motion. Motion is running in place without going anywhere, and progress is running from one place to the next. Vision is your road map to your destination.

So let's look further and understand this practically. If a vision is to materialize, you must turn it into a goal. A goal will consist of two major factors:

1. Timeline: How long will it take?

2. Sacrifice or Cost: What will it cost? Let's equate this:

    Vision + Timeline + Cost = Goal Achieved

E.g. Mario wants to start a business. Mario has always envisioned himself owning his own Italian restaurant. Let's equate this:

Vision (Restaurant) + Timeline (7 Months) + Cost ($100,000) = Goal Achieved (Italian Restaurant)

However, let's take one of these factors out of the equation. Let's take the cost factor out:

Vision (restaurant) + Timeline (7months) = You would have poor Mario wondering about a restaurant instead of paying the price to have a restaurant.

Note: Every goal has a price tag, and in this case, if there is no cost, then it's just fantasy.

Let's try a different angle. Let's take the timeline factor out of the equation:

Vision (Restaurant) + Cost ($100,000) = You have Mario establishing his restaurant maybe in 7 months, maybe in 12 months, maybe in 15 months, or maybe never.

Note: The timeline isolates the vision to a matter of time. If the timeline is not met, then there is a natural frustration that occurs, which is good.

Do you see how the equation works?

Many have experienced the benefit of a vision taken seriously—the value of Henry Ford's vision of a vehicle and how it has evolved to this day is well over in the billions. Look at the value of Abraham Lincoln's Emancipation Proclamation, which established an end to slavery; it has brought freedom to many. In both instances, we all live with the value of these two men's vision taken seriously. Understand it takes time, sacrifice, and most of all it takes courage. Never underestimate the value and the power of a vision. Remember, "Vision is the ability to see the end from the beginning; it gives reality to our future."

Number Two on the Road to Your Destination is PERCEPTION

Your **perception** determines your destination—it's not so much what you see, it's how you see it and how you see it can affect your future. If you see your life unhappy, then your marriage will be unhappy, your job will be unhappy, and eventually your outlook on the days to come will be unhappy.

There are so many things in this world that fight for our attention from music, entertainment, media, etc., and those things create thoughts, which can create a mind-set, which can lead into a lifestyle. Have you ever heard, "Whatsoever a man thinketh so he is."? In other words, "What you are today is what you thought yesterday." It's important to screen your mind with thoughts that can help you and not disable you.

In the Bible you find that God's People were about to take the land that God so promised they could have, but before entering, there was a group of men that went in to spy out the land. Upon their return, they were to report on what they saw. When they came back, they reported two reports. The first report was a good report of how they can take the land; the second report was a bad report of how they can't take the land. As both reports were told to the people, the people gravitated to the bad report. In comment, they said, "We are like grasshoppers in their sight." They perceived that they couldn't take the land based upon how they saw themselves in their sight. That day their destiny changed. They didn't take the land. It was forfeited due to a wrong perception of how they saw themselves.

In my own life, I didn't have the greatest beginning. I grew up in a drug environment with parents on drugs. For a portion of my life, I grew up in the foster system, so I dealt with rejection in my life. However, I came to a place in my life that my perception of how I saw myself had to change if I was going to get anywhere. I had to change how I saw myself. How you see yourself today is how you will be tomorrow. So make the conscious choice to change how you see yourself. Remember, "Your **perception** determines your destination."

Number Three on the Road to Your Destination is PROCESS

In my opinion, you can't talk about destiny without talking about process. Unfortunately, we live in a generation that neglects process .Today's generation has a microwave mentality that wants everything now and when it's not done now, they give up on the process. The process consists of a series of actions, changes, and refinements that bring about certain results. Most beginnings are small but never despise the days of small beginnings. Wine would not be wine unless it went through the process of fermentation.

When I look at the Olympics, I am amazed at the life stories of these Olympians, because behind them was a process to get them to the place of where they are today. "Process leads to preparation" and depending on how good you prepared will lead to promotion. A good example of this is found in the Bible when a young man by the name David faced off against Goliath. Though the odds were against David, there was victory on his behalf. See little did Goliath know but David up until that moment was in preparation by battling and defeating a lion and bear. As you know, David defeated Goliath "David's preparation lead to promotion," and the outcome was victory against his enemy and promotion in the life of David. After that day, David's life was never the same.

On the road to your destination, recognize potential process blockers—anything that will cause a delay instead of help. It could be people, circumstances, or past mistakes. I've seen so many people with evident ability and gifts to become great at what they do, but I've also seen those same people blocked from fulfilling purpose because of past negativity. Be aware of the following: As memory deals with the past, imagination deals with the future. Don't make the mistake of letting the shortcomings, failures, or mistakes disable your future because of a negative past memory. Learn from them but don't be lead by them. Here is an example—a young woman can see herself owning her own business, but she's had two other businesses and they've both failed. If she let's her memory of past failures contaminate the future of a new business idea, she will never experience the reality of another business. Be committed to the process. Remember, "The process consists of a series of actions, changes, and refinements that bring about certain results."

Number Four on the Road to Your Destination is Identify your Helps

On the road to your destination, you will find out that it takes a series of helps. Money is a help; Time is a help; Education is a help; People (right association) are a help; Mentorship is a help; Vehicle is a help, etc. It takes a series of helps to get a college degree from possible financial aid, professors, possible tutors, text books, etc. It also takes a series of helps to have optimum health from vitamins, check up from a doctor, working out, eating right, etc., however, beware of pride. It is the enemy of your help. By accepting the notion that you don't need help, you could cause delay and the possible reality of never reaching your destination. Remember, "Identify your Helps."

Number Five on the Road to Your Destination is Ownership

Own before you occupy. I'm reminded of Joshua that knew his destination was to inherit a land that God promised. Before he physically saw the land, he owned the promise in his mind and in his heart. Even upon entering the Promised Land, Joshua faced many battles but through everything, he was convinced of what belonged to him, and it caused him to occupy. As for you, no matter what you may battle in life, don't give up on what you know is yours. Remember, "Own before you Occupy."

In closing, I hope these FIVE KEYS help you on your destination to reaching your purpose. Whether you know it or not, you are going somewhere, so take some time to evaluate the direction of your life.

THE FIVE KEYS TO LIVE BY

- Vision is the ability to see the end from the beginning.
- Your perception determines your destination.
- Process consists of a series of actions, changes, and refinements that bring about certain results.
- Identify your helps.
- Own before you occupy.

David Diaz is an outstanding speaker, trainer, and ordained minister, traveling all over the world conducting seminars on the importance of destiny. He is on the cutting edge of business development and is available for both speaking engagements and guest appearances. David Diaz can be contacted at:

reachingyourpurpose@yahoo.com
(626) 222-8713.

Chapter 5

Is Your Subconscious Mind Your Ally or Enemy?

Glen Curry

You've got it! You've got what it takes to succeed! It's in you!

The power and ability to win, to prosper, to succeed, to be fulfilled, and happy in life is within you. There is an undiscovered champion with tremendous resources within you.

You may not know that there's a winner in you, and that you've got what it takes; but the truth is—you've got it.

Within you is a sort of living *"machine"* that was given to you at birth. This living *machine* has great wisdom and creative power that can absolutely cause you to win in life.

This *machine* has the assignment and capacity to help you achieve all of your goals and materialize the very desires of your heart.

The downside is that if this magnificent *machine* is not guarded, or if it is abused, it will absolutely cause you to lose in life.

This *machine,* therefore, is either your greatest ally or your worst enemy.

This powerful part of our human makeup is referred to by the scientific community as "the subconscious mind." The Bible refers to this part of man as "the inner man or the hidden man of the heart." The Bible further commands us to "be strengthened with all might in the inner man." (Not weakened and without might in your inner man.)

The hard, cold fact of life is that the vast majority of people (which may include you) have unconsciously and ignorantly abused this tremendous ally, both by neglect, and by feeding it harmful, untrue, and disempowering information. Every time you said words like, "I can't, I'm not worthy, I'm undeserving, I'll never get ahead," or similar negative words, you misused and poisoned your own subconscious mind.

That being true, the great news is that you can rewrite your life script. You can change your story. You can begin today to clean out the harmful, poisonous information that is in the process of preparing to manifest in your life in the form of frustration and failure.

You can begin today to "on purpose" feed your subconscious with fuel that will provide the horsepower to produce prosperity, success, and fulfillment in your life.

In my teen years, like so many misdirected Americans, I became involved with drugs and alcohol. I never imagined that I would ever travel the world, be on radio, and own property in Southern California, Maui, and the Bahamas.

Well into my twenties, I had a loser's mentality. I thought in terms of being the victim, not the victor. I had no idea how to materialize the desires of my heart or how to prosper. I seemed doomed to receive only the leftovers that life dished out to me.

One day, out of sheer boredom, I picked up and began reading a self-improvement book. I was surprised to discover, at least according to the book, that my own belief system and the very things I thought and spoke on a regular basis, were disempowering my life. I have to tell you that it's not easy to change a lifetime of negative thinking, but it is possible. The books I began to read mentored and motivated me to make the changes I needed to make.

For my own personal and private use, I began to develop teachings, books, cassette tapes, and affirmation cards that I used daily to accelerate my transformation. My goal was to feed my subconscious mind with life-empowering principles that would work themselves out in actual prosperity, success, and happiness. I shared the principles of victory and success that I was learning with my friends, and as a result, they too began to prosper and enjoy life.

That was many years ago, but to this day, I still read my success and prosperity affirmation cards (of course, there are now several volumes and they are beautifully typeset), and I still listen to my prosperity tape (of course, now it's a CD) as I drive and when I sleep (of course, I try not to sleep when I drive).

Have A Rebellion!!!

It is a known, scientific fact that the subconscious mind will produce in actual circumstances the information that is fed into it on a regular basis. Every day, society in general is attempting to feed our subconscious minds with failure, fear, and insecurity. We must rebel and take control of what we hear, think, and say.

Every parent, teacher, coach, boss, friend, or enemy whoever told you that you are a loser, a failure, or dunce has negatively impacted your subconscious, thus diminishing your ability to prosper and succeed.

To make matters worse, if you are in the habit of negative self talk, which means you sub-vocalize or say negative things about yourself under your breath, you are undermining your own success and future.

Let's consider the rattlesnake. A rattlesnake has fangs that inject venom or poison into its prey. The purpose of the poison is self-defense and survival. To the rattlesnake, its fangs and poison are assets enabling it to kill or immobilize small rodents for food.

Now imagine what would become of the rattler if everyday it bit and injected a small amount of venom into itself. What was given to the rattlesnake as a benefit would soon become the cause of its demise.

In like manner, your subconscious mind was given to you to protect you, to provide for you, and to help you win in every area of your life. However, the same subconscious mind that was given to you to benefit and bless your life, if used improperly, can become like the snake biting itself. It will lead to your demise.

Your subconscious mind works like a copy machine. Whether you know it or not, you have replicated in your life what you put into the *machine* of your subconscious mind.

As a silly prank, some people have pulled down their pants and sat on the glass of a copy machine, making copies of their rear ends.

The very same copy machine can copy the "Declaration of Independence" or a fool's naked rear end. It doesn't matter to the copier. All it is designed to do is to reproduce what is put inside it.

This is how your subconscious mind also works. It doesn't know right or wrong, good or evil, profit or loss. All it is designed to do is to reproduce in actual circumstances what it is fed.

What you feed your subconscious mind through words of repetition and repeated thoughts is what your subconscious mind thinks you want to experience. Remember, it doesn't know the difference between good or bad, it only knows that the information you feed it is what you want to experience.

Feed your subconscious mind fear, worry, doubt, self pity, and losing thoughts, and your subconscious will get busy attempting to attract calamity and loss into your life.

If, on the other hand, you begin feeding your subconscious mind success principles, goals, dreams, and desires, your subconscious will work behind the scenes to cause you to experience the success, prosperity, and happiness that you desire. It's your ally or enemy—you choose by what you say, think, and hear most often.

Stop Building a Case Against Yourself!!!

Almost every person I meet has been building a case against themselves for years. Almost everyone has the false belief that they are too young, too old, too educated, too uneducated, too unworthy, too unlucky, and too late to succeed and prosper. Any excuse will do.

Today, those who do desire to win in life are discovering that to succeed the proper way, they need to develop good character and excellence. Therefore, many work everyday on their behavior in an attempt to become "a better person." This doesn't work in the long run.

My number one goal for mentorship, whether with a single client or before a large audience, is to persuade those wanting to live life to the fullest, to work *not on their behavior,* but on their thought life, which affects both their conscious and subconscious minds, which ultimately and permanently improves behavior. (Wrong behavior is a manifestation or symptom of wrong thinking.)

It's your thoughts that create your feelings and ultimately your actions as well.

A very important step towards achieving your dream is to ask yourself, "What's occupying my thought life most of the day?" It is important to honestly think about what you are thinking about, because what you think about, you bring about.

Become a Blessing Magnet!!!

The Biblical character, Job, experienced tragedy and then explained the principle I'm sharing with you. "The thing which I greatly feared is come upon me, and that which I was afraid of is come unto me" (Job 3:25).

Job admitted that he attracted tragedy, calamity, and loss into his life by mentally dwelling on wrong, fearful thoughts.

If the story of Job is true, and I believe it is, then the opposite side of the same coin is also true. If you can attract trouble into your life by thinking negative, then you can attract success, victory, prosperity, good heath, favor, and happiness into your life by mentally dwelling on profitable thoughts. Wrong thoughts attract failure; right thoughts attract blessings. It's as simple as that.

It's time to put an end to your insignificant, so-so, mediocre life. There's still time to thrive while you're alive.

It's not too late to be all that you are capable of being!

An extraordinary, sensational life full of happiness, accomplishment, and joy unspeakable awaits you!

The first step is getting rid of the unproductive "stinking thinking" which has held you back and contributed to an insignificant, second-rate life.

By purposely feeding your subconscious mind (your creative *machine*) words of faith, power, victory, love, success, and favor, you will transcend the ordinary and become extraordinary in any given field of endeavor.

Your subconscious mind never sleeps, is not lazy, has no limitations, and wants to work for you. Your responsibility is to make this incredible *gift* clearly understand your goals and desires.

Remember! Your subconscious mind assumes that what you talk about, think about, and hear on a regular basis is what you want performed for you—good or bad.

This explains the importance of thinking and speaking positive and eliminating fear and worry from your life.

By forcefully repeating, with persuasion and emotion, words that clearly define your goals and desires, you can cause your subconscious mind to understand what you really want.

Armed with this new, consistent input of power words and thoughts, your subconscious will draw on forces not available to the conscious mind and cause your desires to be materialized. You will begin to do a thousand subtle things different everyday that will draw to you the opportunities and success you desire and deserve.

Like a gun that can save your life or kill your best friend, the subconscious doesn't judge, it just performs and creates. It's time to get it to help you create the top-notch life you were intended to live.

Years ago Napoleon Hill stated, "What the mind can conceive and believe, it can achieve."

You can achieve the accomplishments you've only dreamed about. There is a way, but you can't go into it half hearted. It's going to require persistence and diligence and change, but you can do it.

You must go to work today, right now, developing a "success consciousness." You must resist the "failure consciousness" that has perhaps plagued you for years.

You overcome and conquer the "failure consciousness" by decrees and affirmations and statements of what you want and who you want to become.

Stop harboring that negative thought or belief! It's a lot easier to remove a twig from your backyard than it is to remove a full grown oak tree. The sooner you recognize a disempowering thought or belief, the better. Deal with it. Call it for what it is—a lie! Then speak words out loud that destroy and kill the negative thought or belief that you don't want to happen in your life, and speak with all conviction what you do want, in its place.

If the thought surfaces that says, "I'm stupid," you kill that thought by saying, "That's a lie, I'm intelligent!" If your belief system tells you that it is your "lot in life to be poor," speak against that wrong lying belief and say, "That's a lie, I'm destined to do well and prosper!"

As you resist the negative thoughts and beliefs in this way, you are planting new seeds of success into your subconscious mind that will produce a wonderful harvest. Soon your subconscious mind will aid you in carrying out the actions and reactions that will propel you to success. In addition to this, your subconscious mind will begin to communicate with your conscious mind ideas, inspiration, and wisdom that, when acted upon, will produce tremendous results.

It's absolutely true: your only limitation is that which you have set up in your own mind. And now you can remove that limitation by thinking right and speaking right.

The subconscious mind is the source of man's greatest power. It can be influenced to work for you, toward your desired goals, even while you sleep.

The subconscious mind is an invisible friend or foe that helps you to obtain what you think of most often. Whether it is a friend or foe depends on you. What are you feeding it through thoughts and words? What are you listening to on a regular basis? This friend or foe will always help you receive the very thing you are anticipating—good or bad.

I encourage you to believe that the statements presented here concerning your creative *machine* (the subconscious mind) are true.

When you have a fixed goal, a clear picture of your desire always before you (repetition of affirmations that you desire makes this possible), your desire will become buried deeply into your subconscious mind. At that point, as you continue your affirmations of words, thoughts, and mental pictures, your subconscious mind will go to work to help you create the physical equivalent of what at first was only a desire.

Once the subconscious receives your message and clearly understands your desires and ambitions, it will only be a short time before your desires will be fulfilled and your goals and ambitions achieved.

Glen Curry is the founder of "Fine Tuned for Success." He is dedicated to help those who desire a higher level of success find the information, strategy, motivation, and tools they need to win in life. A dynamic public speaker, radio personality, and author, Glen has developed many tools for success. No winner should be without his cards, "Principles of Success for Champions and Winners."

To view or order Glen's life changing materials and tools for victory, success, and prosperity, please visit:
www.finetunedforsuccess.com

Glen can be contacted at:
glencurry@finetunedforsuccess.com

Chapter 6

Bill Bailey Speaks Out On Network Marketing
"An Exclusive One on One"

Bill Bailey

Who is William E. Bailey? He is the mentor of mentors of all time. From his humble beginnings as one of 11 children raised in the hills of Kentucky, this amazing man has accomplished more in his lifetime than most men could accomplish in 50 lifetimes. From that humble beginning, Bill Bailey earned his BA from the University of Illinois and traveled all over the world building businesses, the largest in its peak grossed over $64 million dollars per month. Mr. Bailey has flown his own personal Sabre Jet, sailed his 110' yacht, and lived the lifestyle of the rich and famous. He has performed in Shakespearean plays, on television, successfully promoted a World lightweight Boxing Championship, and had a personal audience in 1968 with Pope Paul VI who recognized him for his philanthropic efforts on behalf of the orphans in San Jose.

Yes, this is a mentor you want to learn from and reap from his wisdom. Mr. Bailey is a legend in the field of personal development and team building. He has mentored and trained such greats as Jim Rohn, Les Brown, Larry Thompson, Willie Larkin, and many others. In 1972, Mr. Bailey, along with Ross Perot and Ray Kroc, received the coveted Horatio Alger Award personally presented by Dr. Norman Vincent Peale "for distinguished service to youth, enhancing the

American traditions of individual initiative, perseverance, integrity, and love for freedom".

Now that you know who Bill Bailey is let's tap into his mentorship as Bill Bailey speaks out.

Don: Mr. Bailey, thank you for taking the time to share with us your insights and wisdom. Since we want to learn all we can, I want to jump right in and ask you, "When you first started in business, did you believe you were going to be a multi-millionaire?"

Bill: No I did not. I had come from a working class mindset, and when I first got involved with network marketing, I saw this as an opportunity to earn a few hundred dollars extra a month. I started out part time and built my way up. But, partner, I found out that you could become rich in this industry. I worked with two other network marketing companies before I started my own. What I did have when I first started out was a vision of a better life, and from there I built up.

Don: Why do so many fail to climb the "Millionaire Mountain"?

Bill: The first reason is many people refuse to leave their comfort zone. They have the fear of the unknown. They base their decisions of their future on their past. Our culture and world is based on change, so in order for us to grow, we must change. Fear is the greatest hindrance to mankind. It blocks their God-given potential, and stops them from believing in themselves. Fear causes people to accept less than what they can have. Eighty percent of all people I have ever met in my life have far more ability than they think they have. The next thing people do is give up on themselves. They settle for so little when so much is available and that, in my opinion, is why so many fail to climb the "Millionaire Mountain." For instance, if you just allow yourself to dream, you can accomplish just about anything you set your mind to. From my small beginnings on a farm in Kentucky, I have had the good fortune to have lunch with Mr. Armstrong just 6 months after coming home from the moon. What an amazing event that was to have him share with me his amazing journey. Then, in the 60's, I had the opportunity to buy a bunch of toys, which I gave to a group of orphans in San Jose. There were about 3,000 children, and I spent $94,000 on them. The money was not the important thing; it was about helping them and what a joy it brought me to see those children light up with smiles. Because of that act, the Pope found out about it, and I got to have a private and personal meeting with him. This and many other wonderful things I have had the privilege to experience, to me, shows proof positive that there is no shortage in life.

Don: From your perspective Mr. Bailey, why are mentors so important?"

Bill: From the beginning of time, everything we have learned was taught to us by someone else. Mentors teach us the pathway to success. However, you must make sure your mentor has done the things he is teaching you, not just talked about them. They must have walked the path themselves. A mentor acts as your friend and can see your inner potential. They help you find the track of success, and then help you stay on it. Mentors cannot give you talents, what they can do is take the talents you do have and help you develop them. They work with us giving us the direction, encouragement, and pressure we need to make our dreams come true. Everything in the universe is designed to grow. I look around and I see the trees growing, I see my animals growing, I see my grandchildren growing, and if we are not growing, then we are going backwards. Mentors help us to continually grow, to stretch, and move forward.

They help us learn how to live—really live. I retired twice and I will never do that again. When you learn to find your passion, it's not work. For someone who works in their passion, for him or her to retire is like giving an unemployed man a vacation. Mentors are very important if not mandatory to our success.

Don: You built one of the most powerful network marketing companies in the industry, at its peak generating $64 million dollars a month. "What are 4 secrets to becoming successful in network marketing?"

Bill:

1. You must find a company that has a demonstrable value. If you are lucky, you will find one that everyone can use and benefit from. If you have the right product and a system to teach personal self-development, you have a winning team.

2. You must realize it will take time to develop the skills to become proficient in network marketing, and that is why personal development and having mentors are so important.

3. You must have a proper mindset. You must make up your mind that this is going to be your career and vehicle to reach your financial goals. You must have the mindset that you will not quit; that you will not be overcome with the negative feelings or difficult circumstances that come your way.

4. You must have a total commitment to you and your future—a commitment to climb that mountain. If someone tells you, "It's hot," say, "Good, I will get my shorts," or "It's raining," say, "Good, I'll grab my rain coat," or "The climb is slippery," say, "Good, I'll get on my hands and crawl." In other words, you get totally committed in advance to find out what you need to do to climb that mountain, and then be committed to do it. Remember you cannot control people. The only one you can control is you.

Mr. Bailey, thank you once again for taking the time to share and mentor our readers on the fine art of success and achievement.

Sign up for a Free 30-Minute Mentoring Session with William E. Bailey or Dr. Karen O'Donnell—it will be a life-changing experience. The concept behind our approach to personal mentoring is simple, but quite profound in the results achieved.

Just go to www.williamebailey.com

Chapter 7

Pursuing Men Of Briar

George Ramirez

This is an excerpt from George Ramirez' latest book soon to be released.

Briar: A hardy tough wood that is actually a tap root that supplies nourishment to treelike shrubs. They withstand heat, drought, fire, chopping, and extreme adversity. Actually, the wood is so tough, it has been carved into pipes for smoking tobacco. The older it gets, the smoother the smoke and the more valuable it becomes—just like the men in this book.

Dedicated to three men of briar—my father, my father-in-law, and my brother.

"When the student is ready, the teacher will appear." We've all heard this, but it is the way of the mentorship process. Many times, in our busy lives, we pass up or are passed up by opportunities to be mentored or at least guided through an unknown part of our journey.

We hustle and bustle and zoom through traffic listening to our self-help CDs, attend countless seminars, and maybe even pay for personal coaching. So what if in our quest for polished, sophisticated, maybe even expensive mentoring, we aren't paying attention to what is right before us! You know—the forest for the trees and all that.

One of the greatest sources of wisdom and amazing commonsense are old people! Yep, the slower moving, overly wrinkled, usually very eccentric (and many times should never be driving) senior crowd.

Now don't get all politically correct on me, this has nothing to do with geriatric prejudice. Old people got old by doing some things right, and they have seen things we haven't. You can learn by experience or by wisdom. You can jump the fence yourself and personally live through getting bit by "Hercules" or you can watch your friend get bit—this is wisdom. You choose.

What follows is just one example that re-enforces the benefits of being quiet and just listening—really listening.

One magical day, three amazing men, seated on CD's patio, were enjoying a beautiful summer afternoon in the mountains, sipping beer, soda, and huge amounts of nostalgia. All three had proudly served in the American military during WWII, two were Navy and one was Army. The average age of the trio was now 73. Each had married their childhood sweetheart and was still trying to figure them out decades later.

Each was incredibly resourceful, had lived through the depression, understood commitment, and truly stood by their word.

These men of such humbling straight grain also had their quirks. Each used and hated their glasses, two walked with a limp but never complained—unless it helped them get out of a job the wife requested. And to make it really interesting, they could tell stories, all at the same time! You see each one had only one good ear, and that afternoon, we were seated in a way that I was in the middle with all the bad ears facing each other.

Here's what I learned:

1) It was pretty much agreed upon that I was too young to know my #%* from a hole in the ground, so it would do me good to sit there and listen. I figured I was outnumbered, so I sat there.

2) Each one's childhood, sports, wartime, or work-related injuries were worse than the previous guy's…until it was his turn to talk again.

3) If the mom and the dad spent enough time at home that the kids really knew they were loved, and if they misbehaved, they would get the "tar whuped outta them," they would turn out to be good kids; then they would raise their kids the same way, thereby insuring these three that they would have wonderful grandkids. Sounded pretty self-serving to me, but between them, they had 19 kids and too many grandkids to count, and the large majority of them turned out to be real good.

4) Some of the stories (most of which I had heard before) had changed somewhat since the last telling. Since we were all up in the mountains, I chalked it up to the affects of altitude.

5) Never interrupt!

6) Manuel used to smuggle women's nylons into the U.S. through Mexico after he was discharged. He sold them to American girls to help support his family. They used to pack the nylons into the tires of the cars and drive them back across the border. He could also load up an entire wagon full of firewood so that none of it would fall off while delivering it. He used no ropes!

One of his hobbies and talents was working on cars. While dating his soon-to-be wife, he took apart a Buick and a Cadillac, found a few extra parts, and built a hot rod that went 150 m.p.h. He raced it through the streets of Los Angeles and got busted by the police. When he went to court, the judge said, "Can it really go 150 m.p.h.?" Manuel answered, "It could and did." The judge smiled, nodded, and said, "If you're smart enough to build a car that goes 150 m.p.h. and not crash it, you don't deserve a ticket." Manuel paid an eight dollar court fee and left, with the car.

7) Smitty could place 4 or 5 peanuts into his mouth and chew for a full thirty minutes…and not miss a turn.

8) By now there were times that these three had my head spinning; but one thing was certain, they admired and respected each other. I listened in awe as they shared family experiences. I realized that, even though they came from different family backgrounds, were born 1,000 miles apart from each other, and culturally had very little in common, they had the same core beliefs.

I thought of how many times I had heard that race was such an important issue—so not true. Your character and manner of behavior means so much more. Why spend so much energy looking at the amount of melanin a person has? Spend more time knowing what is on the inside.

9) CD's wife stuck her head out through the screen door, asked if anybody needed anything. Getting no requests, she smiled, looked directly at me, and said, "Well, George, I bet these old men are really giving you an earful." Any answer I gave would have gotten me in a world of hurt. Especially if I said, "Oh yes, ma'am, this is really great," or some other lame remark. I could have ended up spending the night out there on the patio.

Considering how long it took me to finally get the true meaning of what my lessons were for that day, perhaps I would have been better off listening to them all night.

The beer was warm, the soda had lost its fizz, and they were ready for supper. The wives had it ready. I walked back to our cabin and sat down out front and realized that for the last 3½ hours, I had been privileged enough to listen to real history, told by real men who had grabbed life, rolled with its punches, came up swinging, and created success for themselves, their families, and years later, me.

George Ramirez is an outstanding public speaker and trainer, covering business across the nation and being well traveled worldwide. His experience, along with his wit and wisdom, makes him a favorite in every audience. George resides in Whittier, California, along with his beautiful wife and life partner, Olivia Ramirez. He can be contacted at george@gengold.net or by calling (866) 945-4730.

Chapter 8

Discovering Your Champion Within

Dr. Jacqueline Sisson

As I sit ready to put pen to page, I reminisce, with a grateful heart, about the value that mentors have brought to my life. Mentors taught me to believe, to cast aside my limiting beliefs, to give myself permission to dream outside my familiar comfort zone, and to dare to live the life of my dreams. I have had the privilege of sitting and learning from some of the greatest minds in the arena of self-development.

In the beginning I did it alone. In the still of the night, while the world slept, I pressed into the hope of making a better way for my family and myself. I read books, listened to audio tapes and CDs, saved my pennies, and went to every seminar and conference that I could. Daring to borrow their courage, I began to find my way and to embrace unlimited dreams of my own.

The journey of discovering the champion within starts with asking yourself three very important questions.

Who Are You?
Where Are You?
What Are Your Hopes and Dreams?

Who are you? It is my belief we are created tripartite—in three parts.

93

Spirit is the innermost layer of our being. It transcends this world and communes with God or if you prefer you may insert your own belief. Whether we choose to develop our Spirit or not, it impacts our lives. It is the core of our being and when addressed it creates a strong foundation on which to build the life we desire and deserve. Whether you have a belief or are an agnostic, it shapes who you are.

Soul is the second layer. It consists of the mind, will, and emotions. It is a non-tangible part of us that cannot physically be touched but tends to drive most of what we want.

The mind consists of our *thinking* quotient. What we think determines what and who we become. It has been said, "If you think you can or you think you can't, you are probably right." Our *thinking* will either propel us forward toward victories or bog us down into the muck of defeats. A favorite mentor of mine, Charlie Tremendous Jones, said, "You will remain the same five years from now as you are today except for two things, the books you read and the people you meet."

The will is both mysterious and fascinating. It supercedes our emotions and is fueled by its own success. I define it as the strength of our self-determination—the center of our resolve and choice. Both the mind and the will are like our bodies in that the more we exercise them, the stronger they become.

Emotions can range as high as the joy of wonderment at the miracle of birth to as low as the intense sorrow of regret and loss that accompanies the death of a loved one. I refer to our emotions as the spices of life.

Body is our physical shell that houses the other counterparts. Different sizes and shapes—it is up to us how we take care of what we have. I believe in the art of prevention and know the advantage of regular exercise, drinking water daily, and the importance of adding fruits and vegetables to your diet. The American Cancer Society is now recommending 5-9 servings of fruits and vegetables a day. I know the significance but still do not always meet the requirements so I have the next best thing. I have added Juice Plus+ to my diet, the true "Jetson Food" for the 21st Century.

The three—spirit, soul, body—are intricately woven together and each one affects the other.

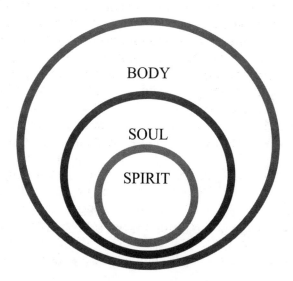

Where are you? It is said "...to everything there is a season, and a time for every matter or purpose under heaven...a time to be born, and a time to die; a time to plant, and a time to pluck up what is planted...a time to kill and a time to heal; a time to break down, and a time to build up…a time to weep and a time to laugh; a time to mourn, and a time to dance….a time to embrace, and a time to refrain from embracing….a time to receive and a time to lose….a time to keep, and a time to cast away…a time to rend, and a time to sew…a time to keep silent, and a time to speak; a time to love, and a time to hate; a time of war, and a time of peace…" As the seasons follow one another in nature so do the seasons of our lives.

Another favorite mentor of mine, Jim Rohn, wrote an entire book on the subject, *The Seasons of Life*. It is a wonderful book and goes into great detail.

How do I describe seasons? Alas *Spring*, a welcome break from the long cold winter. A time to plant not just crops as farmers but to plant seeds of hopes, dreams, and visions you desire for your life. It is a time to anticipate seedlings in your life to begin to take root. A time to plant not only in our lives but also in the lives of others—friends, family, work associates, and those we mentor. Take care to continue to do all that is necessary to reap a harvest of abundance. Whatever we plant in the various aspects of our life—mentally, physically, and spiritually—will take root and begin to blossom.

Summer tends to be dry, so take care. Water regularly and watch guard over the seeds you so carefully planted. Take care not to allow *dream-stealers* to plant weeds of doubt or dismay in your life. Although you may be tempted to kick back and wait for the harvest, you must stay busy continuing the activity that will give you the desired results while preparing for the cold winds of winter.

Autumn is the time you have been waiting for. Now you are able to reap the rewards of all the planting, sowing, watering, and guarding, until the time has come for the harvest. It is a colorful time as the earth makes way for its long winter sleep. It may be that you received that promotion or the recognition that you wanted.

Winter is a dark, cold season. It appears that all is quiet and still, but don't be deceived. Germination is taking place underground. You can't see it but it is. Just trust the process. Through the storms of winter, our pantries will give provision if we have done our due diligence. Maybe you had a disappointment, lost a job, were blindsided by a blow of life, or something that you counted on didn't come through. Know that this is just a season, and if you have done your due diligence in the previous seasons of spring, summer, and fall, spring will come once again.

We cannot pick and choose what season we are in, but we can always choose our attitude. We can always prepare for the dry times and store up for the cold winters.

What are your hopes and dreams? I believe it all starts with hope. It is said that "faith is the substance of things hoped for not yet seen." Are you hoping for things in your life to change? For this change to occur, what is your responsibility? Keep in mind that for things to change—*I must change*. "I" is the most essential part.

I believe that without a vision, we are sure to sit in the arena of mediocrity and watch as life simply passes us by. What are your goals and dreams? Are you living the life of your dreams? Or, are you, like so many others, simply waiting for the big break to come without taking action? Quite honestly, in all my years of coaching and mentoring, I very seldom see the big break come without the person making a decision to take action.

Surround yourself with *dream-catchers* and do away with dream-stealers. Dream-catchers are our mentors. I have my favorites, and I will share them with you later, but discover the ones that best resonate with who you are and where you want to go.

Dream-catchers are those that believe in you, sometimes family, friends, and angels unaware. You may be sitting there thinking, *Well, I don't have anyone.* If that is true, then NOW is the time for YOU to take action and press into the arena of self growth. Erase all former excuses as to WHY your big break hasn't come and take advantage of the opportunities before you now. The library is one of the most valuable resources for information. It is filled with mentors waiting for you to open their books and feast on the knowledge therein. Make a decision to invest in yourself. I have a library at home of books, CDs, and DVDs filled with life-changing information.

Turn away from dream-stealers. You can recognize them by how you feel when you finish talking with them. They are people in your life that remind you of who you are not. These people are poison to the mind, body, and spirit. They steal any hope of you creating a foundation for the life you desire and deserve.

Another aspect of dream-stealing often goes unnoticed. It is the dream-stealer within—silent but deadly. This dream-stealer is your own limiting beliefs that come as a thief in the night to remind you of your own doubts, fears, limitations, and past failures.

Dare to dream. So many times we are not allowed to dream nor taught how to dream. If you could do or be anything you want in your life, what would you do, and what would you be? What are your deep desires? What do you long for? It is never too late. What I didn't realize was that many things I desired and wanted were not just about me but about my purpose here at this moment and time.

It is all up to you—BELIEVE. If I can do it, you can too. Jim Rohn says, "Let others live ordinary lives, but not you." I believe you have a champion within just waiting to be unleashed. Find that champion and begin your journey of discovery and follow your dreams. An abundance of possibilities lie in wait for you to embrace them. Make them yours and live. All things are possible—BELIEVE!

Our first mentors were our parents or whoever raised us. As children, we assumed their truths and core beliefs as our own, as we had no other reference point.

My first mentor was my father, a man of great honor and integrity. He was a country preacher who lived what he preached and taught me many lessons that have impacted my life. Two lessons he taught me were to have a healthy respect and love for God, and to treat others with the same dignity and respect as I would like to be treated.

I remember when I was small, I would go to town with Daddy, and he would say hello and smile to each person that passed by. At the time, I thought he must know everyone in the world. Later he would teach me the valuable lesson that it is just as easy to go the extra mile and be kind and greet others with a smile, because it may be the only smile they had that entire day.

When looking for a mentor, find one that resonates with your core beliefs. I chose my mentors very carefully. Foremost, I looked for integrity. Some of my favorite mentors have been Jim Rohn, Denis Waitley, Zig Ziglar, Charlie Tremendous Jones, and Dr. John Gray.

Victor or Victim—it is your choice. Each step of my journey has taught me valuable life lessons that could not have been learned any other way. Whether I am in the winter, spring, summer, or fall, each step has led me to the path I am on today.

Let's take a snapshot inventory. Give yourself a score from 1-10 for each item below:

1 = needs the most work
10 = completely satisfied with where you are

- Are you spiritually connected?
- Are you feeding your spirit regularly (in accordance with your personal belief)?
- Do you believe in you?
- Do you feed your mind positive, uplifting material?
- Do emotions get in the way of where you want to be?
- Do you have limiting beliefs that keep you from reaching your full potential?

- Do you exercise regularly?
- Do you eat the 5-9 recommended servings of fruits and vegetables each day?
- Do you drink water (8-10 glasses a day)?
- Are you comfortable with your body?
- How would you rate your relationships?
- What is your relationship with your spouse or significant other?
- What is your relationship with your friends?
- What is your relationship with your family?
- What is your relationship with your work associates?
- Do you enjoy your work environment?
- How would you rate your goals?
- How would you rate your life balance?
- How would you rate your financial well-being?
- How would you rate your preparation for retirement?
- How would you rate your vacation choices?
- How would you rate your dreams?
- How would you rate your vision?
- Are you living the life you desire?

The purpose of this inventory is to show you precisely where you are today in the various categories of your life. Understand this is just the beginning.

This is your guide for "next step thinking and growth." Find a mentor. Find several. Know that a journey begins with one step. Today is your day. Take that step. Maybe you already are on your own path of self development. BRAVO! Continue to grow, change, and be all that you can be. Let me know how you're doing. I would love to hear from you.

Personal Note:
Today, I am blessed beyond measure, in every way. I have been married to my soul-mate Larry for 35 years. We have two grown, married children, and recently we had the incredible joy of becoming grandparents to Kylee Marie Barnes. She is the light of our lives! From my meager beginning, who would have thought that I would be experiencing the amazing success I am today. BELIEVE—all things are possible!

If I can serve you in any way, don't hesitate to contact me and share.

Dr. Jacqueline Sisson, A.T. is known as Dr. JAS "Heart Specialist." She is an ordained minister, has a Ph.D. in Psychology, and is currently pursuing a Ph.D. in Homeopathic Nutrition. Dr. Sisson is a Business and Personal Coach for Jim Rohn International. Dr Sisson has been involved on the cutting edge of the personal growth arena for over 25 years. A dynamic international speaker, she has what it takes to bring out the very best in the lives she touches. A Keynote, International Speaker, Personal/Business Coach, she can be reached at:

Dr. Jacqueline Sisson, A.T.
San Diego, CA
Office: (619) 691-1954
Fax: (619) 691-1951
Cell: (619) 993-4607
Email: allthat772@aol.com
Website: www.atouchofhealthbyjacqueline.com

Chapter 9

Partner With A Leader

Melinda Boyer
"Sunshine"

Take a look at your partner and ask yourself, "Is he or she a giant in faith, a true leader?" If the answer is yes, you need to decide if you are willing to go alone or if you can be a whole-hearted partner in the adventures in your lives together.

Life will always want us to look back. But in reality, we are holding our family and partners from moving forward every time we turn our heads back. KEEP MOVING FORWARD! When we start to manipulate and connive, we are missing out on what our adventures with our partners can really be. When we are compassionate with our partners, who are like minded, our skills become sharpened and refined, and we find ourselves doing things we never thought were possible. We actually start enjoying the things we thought we wouldn't enjoy. So step back and think this out. Being a partner with a leader is a commitment with a price to pay, but also comes with great rewards.

It is always easier to look at the things we don't have, but stop and take a look at what you do have and be thankful for it. This is a key to living successfully with someone who is a leader.

"Don't just be a partner—be a partner with adventure!"

103

We all have lost something in our lives and didn't think we could ever bounce back. You become so blinded by what is going on around you and everyone around you is telling you to snap out of it! Wake up! Have you ever said that to someone? You just want to slap them! Believe me, my kids wanted to do that to me several times. I was like that for about 2 years— walking around like a zombie. Until one day I woke up and really understood that I could do better if I would just move forward.

You see you will always be where you are until you take off the blinders and really dig deep in yourself and pull it out, and start moving on it. When you start to go for what you want, change will come with it. And if you are not willing to change, you will always be where you are now. Work on you! No one else will do if for you. Only you can do it for you.

When I first met my husband, I thought he was a dream or something. I thought for sure no man really existed that still actually opened the car door for you. I thought those men only existed in the early 1900's. Before we got married he told me, I won't try to change you if you don't try to change me. But you work on you for me, and I will work on me for you. I was in complete shock when I heard that. No one had ever told me that. The first thing that came to my mind was, "Is this guy for real?" At that point I understood— you can't change people but you can change yourself. That's when our marriage really blossomed like a beautiful bouquet of roses. He is a true leader, my mentor, and teacher.

Sometimes we need to take a step back and look at things with an open mind. If you are going into a marriage or are in a marriage and your partner is in leadership or is thinking about going into some kind of leadership role, you better have a workable spirit and have an open mind to learn new things. I know some women can be very selfish and stubborn, and that is why I believe there are so many women now that are leaving their husbands. Women begin to see them selves as the leader in the home and most women will say, "If I am doing everything myself, then why do I need him." Well let me tell you, sister, you will find out you are not that leader you really thought you were when you are forced to become one by yourself. And then you will have a rude awakening. You see, you will want to take a step back and realize that it is not just about you but about the both of you, working as a team.

There are times when I want to just scream at my husband, "HELLO? What about me!" And I do sometimes. Then I realize, wait a minute, he does make time for me. But I want ALL his time. Now tell me ladies, do you not get like that sometimes? But there is one thing that I have come to understand for both men and women, if you give them the time and space that they need, they will give you the time that you need. Your relationship and understanding for one another will be so much better. That is when you start to understand the principle of successful partnership.

Learn to have more understanding with each other, learn to relax, and enjoy your life. When you give yourself a time-out, you will be so much better for yourself and others. I was one to always say forget this, I don't need this, and storm out of the house. Until one day I realized, man, what am I running for and where am I going? I was so tired of running. Trust me, running will never get you anywhere.

Here are some simple Do's and Don'ts:

Do's	Don'ts
Devotion	Temptation
Loyalty	Selfishness
Believe in your Partner	Manipulate
Faith	Connive
Understanding	Jealousy
Compassion	Envy
Give	
Respect	

Learn principles and put boundaries in your life. These are the things that I have learned by being a partner with a leader. Look for balance and strive for going forward and don't look back.

If you feel you are called to leadership but really don't understand what you are getting into, let me tell you, you could be asking for something you know nothing about. Look for what you think you can achieve and what really gives you peace and makes you happy. Look at what you would like to achieve in your life and realize it might take a while to get there. Understand that when you look at something you really would like to achieve, it won't just be handed to you. There are steps that you must take to get there, and most people are not willing to take those steps.

Apply yourself and learn to put disciplines in your life. If you really want to be a leader and be a Partner of a Leader, you will have to apply certain disciplines to achieve success, harmony, and peace. This will apply to you as well as your partner.

"Be Careful What You Ask For"

I have always wanted to be with someone who knows what they want and knows exactly where they are going. But one thing I didn't realize is there are challenges to face. When you are with someone who has dreams, inspirations, and insight of where they are going, you better be prepared to follow right beside them and be willing to go through whatever comes their way. Leaders have a different paradigm than most people. You will have to go through the mood swings, ups, downs, and long hours. Most of them can't stop thinking. They are always thinking of the next project, the next thing they have to focus on, the next meeting to go to, what people they have to meet with next, or how something works. You definitely need to be up for the challenge and adventure.

If you are single and looking for that special someone who is on stage or is in a leadership roll, you better be careful what you are asking for or you just might get it. Be aware, when you see a leader up on stage or in a leadership role, it is very easy to get infatuated with the deception of that seemingly "Glorious Life." What you don't see is the price that is so expensive. No one could pay it unless you were truly "called" into leadership and called to be a partner to a leader.

I honor all the ladies who are successfully standing beside their husbands, supporting them, and being a partner right along side them. You don't necessarily have to be on stage with them, that may not be your cup of tea, but you are with them up there in your heart and support. This ladies is one key to being a "partner with a leader".

Melinda Boyer is an up and coming speaker and writer. She is the co-founder of Real Life Teaching and Real Life Publishing along with her husband Don Boyer. She is the mother of 3 wonderful children, Manuel, Marco and Marina and a beautiful new granddaughter "Mariah". Visit Melinda at melindaboyer@realifeteaching.com.

Chapter 10

The Greatest Success We'll Know Is Helping Others Succeed and Grow

Greg S. Reid

Let's face it—work stinks! Unless, of course, you love what you do.

Wouldn't it be great to have passion toward your life and career and make a positive impact on the world in which you live?

People just like you, who want more out of their lives, spend *millions* of dollars each year on self-improvement books, tapes, CDs, and other paraphernalia, only to end up exactly where they began. Do you know why? It's simple, really. They're missing the key ingredient of all great success stories—a mentor.

All the "boom shacka lacka" motivational pep talks in the world will do little good if they only *tell* you what to do. You need something more. You need a mentor to *show* you how to do what you desire.

When you learned how to ride a bike, you probably didn't do it by reading a book or listening to a CD. If you're like most people, you learned when you were a kid, with your mom or dad running alongside and helping you keep your balance until you got the hang of it. Just as reading a pamphlet wouldn't teach you everything you need to know about riding a bike, listening to motivational CDs won't teach you everything about growing and succeeding in life. You need someone to take you by the hand—and the seat of your pants—and show you how to do it.

When the Student Is Ready, the Teacher Will Appear

There's an old saying that you've probably heard a thousand times: *When the student is ready, the teacher will appear.* What does this mean, exactly? It means that your teachers and mentors are right in front of you at all times, and when you're ready to learn the lessons they have to share, they'll suddenly pop into view.

Many refer to this by the fancy term *reticular activating system* or RAS. Here's how it works. Suppose you've just driven away from a car dealership in your brand-new red Honda. Suddenly; you're amazed to see how many other red Hondas are all around you. Did they just magically appear? Of course not. They were there all the time. However, it was not until you began to focus your attention on red Hondas that your eyes began to notice them.

Mentorship works in much the same way. Once you realize that you need or desire some guidance in your life—*poof!* Out of the blue, those mentors suddenly show themselves, and you realize they were there all along.

By the way, did you know it's okay to have many mentors in your life? Absolutely! It's highly useful to have mentors in many different avenues of your life—one for your personal relationships, one for business and finance, and another for fitness, just to offer an example.

Traits and Qualities of a Great Mentor

Now here's the big question: What is a mentor, and what should you look for when seeking one? First, please know that a mentor is not a counselor or a therapist. Mentors are there to guide you and offer direction, not to be used as an emotional dumping ground. Mentors don't have to have all the answers, but they do need to be able to point you in the right direction so you can find the answers that your mentor doesn't have.

A mentor is a confidant, someone you can trust and confide in. One important note is that you should seek out a mentor of your own sex, so you can discuss sensitive issues with a like-minded person.

Good mentors have one very important common denominator: They tell you what you need to hear, not just what you want to hear. Great mentors do something that few will ever do—they hold you accountable. That's the sign of a truly fine mentor.

In life it has been said, "We are exactly where we choose to be." A good mentor will ask, "Where are you now? Why did you let yourself get there? Do you want to be somewhere else? Are you willing to do what it takes to get there?" By answering these questions openly, honestly, and in a positive manner, you can help your mentor to take you from where you are to where you want to be.

The secret is to take this information, sit down with your personal guide, and see how you can implement these principles into your current activities in order to gain results. All the information in the world is useless unless it is applied. That's where the power of personal mentorship really kicks in, and where you are tested of your true desires.

Let me tell you a quick story of how I met my mentor.

Some time ago, I decided to put myself up for auction on eBay. I wanted to be the first speaker to do so, and I thought to myself, *Why not?* Spring Air Mattress Corporation was the highest bidder, and all proceeds went to the Big Brothers Big Sisters organization. It was a true win-win right from the beginning.

Spring Air is headquartered in a beautiful part of the country in the heart of Utah. My trip there and the meeting that followed were fantastic; however, it was a mentor I met on the journey who really made a difference in my life and changed the way I viewed success from that day forward. Let me start from the beginning and set the scene.

While staying at the Grand America Hotel, I couldn't help but notice the incredible decorating and workmanship that had gone into this classic masterpiece. I felt like I was in a castle—walking on imported wood floors, surrounded by marble walls, and passing under the finest glass chandeliers I've ever laid eyes on. The only word I can use to describe it is *majestic.* While enjoying a warm cup of refreshment during "high tea," I noticed an elderly gentleman in the corner of the lobby. People were walking up to him, kneeling down to touch his hand, and whispering words into his ear. I thought to myself, *who is this guy—the Pope?*

After querying a few staff members, I learned that his name was Earl Holding, and he was the owner and operator of this great palace, along with the entire Little America hotel chain, which stretched from state to state. Now, anyone who knows me knows what happened next—of course I went over to talk with him.

An hour or so into our meeting, Earl looked at me and said, "You now know more about me than my own children do."

"That's probably because most people want to talk about all the success you have in your life and all the things you possess," I replied, "while I want to learn *how* you created your success so I can duplicate it for myself and teach others to do the same."

"Want to know how I made a fortune?" my new mentor asked.

"Please," I answered.

"Luck and *ACTION,*" he bellowed. "When I was younger, I wanted to get into the oil business, so I bought a used oil rig. Funny thing—I struck oil on the first try, nearly 800 barrels a day, and if you know the oil business, you know that's nearly impossible. I truly was *very* lucky. The point is that I took action to have that luck. If I'd never bought that rig, taken the chance, and popped it into the dirt, I would not have succeeded the way I did. It's like that old quote: The more action you take, the luckier you get."

"Wow," was the most provocative response I could come up with.

"That's nothing!" he shouted back with a hint of laughter. "It's what I did next that made me the man I am today. You see, I took the profits from that first strike and did it again and again, buying more and more rigs until I finally fulfilled my dream and bought one of the largest oil refineries in the nation. Ever hear of Sinclair Oil Corporation?" he asked.

"Of course," I replied. "That's the one with the dinosaur logo, right?"

"That's the one," he responded as he took another sip of his tea. "Now we're producing more oil than I ever dreamed possible."

Our meeting continued and the information flowed as Earl recounted his greatest achievements. I sat there in amazement, listening to story after story as he shared his deepest thoughts. I felt a sense of real appreciation, as if he was passing a baton to an eager student who wanted to do more with his life than he already had.

So, what did I do with this information? Something crazy in today's world, something you don't hear about very often—I *applied* his suggestions. I took action, and what do you know, I made the most money of my life. I guess I was just **lucky**, too!

Mentoring: A Win-Win Situation

We've talked about finding mentors; now let's talk about being a mentor. When you become a mentor to others, you create a win-win situation. Say you worked in an ice cream store and you love ice cream. After all, who doesn't love ice cream? But let's say that you happen to like it more than most people, so you really take your job seriously. When customers walk through the doors, you greet them with a smile and welcome them into the shop. You know them by name and know which flavor they enjoy the most.

Suppose that a few months go by and a new person is hired at the ice cream store. Even though this newbie is green behind the ears, you take him under your wing and teach him the same tricks of the trade you have developed. When guests walk through the door, you introduce them to your new protégé and walk the new hire through the steps to create the patrons' favorite treats.

Now imagine that this goes on for a while, and a new position opens up for a manager's spot. Who do you think they would ask to fill this? You—of course! You've already demonstrated the necessary skills to be a leader. More important than the promotion, though, didn't it feel great to be a mentor and help the newbie feel like part of the team right from the beginning?

That, my friend, is the true power of mentorship. The reason for its success can be found in this little quote: "The greatest success we'll know is helping others succeed and grow."

At the end of the day, when it's all said and done, let me ask you this question. What do you personally enjoy more: your own success or helping others around you succeed?

Can you remember the look on your children's faces when they rode their bikes for the first time on their own? Or later on, when they graduated from school? More than likely, when you reflect back on events in your life, you felt the greatest feelings of pride when other people make great strides around you, not from your own accomplishments. Why? Because the greatest success we'll know is helping others succeed and grow.

Now that you have a full understanding of how this works in both directions, let me offer a little challenge. Take a look around. Turn that reticular activating system on and see what or who surrounds you. Is there a mentor waiting to guide you through life's adventures? Even more important, are you the mentor that someone else is seeking to take them to their own personal oasis?

Go out and make a difference, either way—someone is waiting for you.

Best wishes and whatever you do…

Keep smilin'…

Gregory Scott Reid
#1 Best Selling Author of *The Millionaire Mentor,*
Positive Impact, and *Wake up—Live the Life You Love*

www.AlwaysGood.com

Chapter 11

The Principles to a Productive Vision

Wil Cason

On a warm fall day in Northern California, I woke up anticipating learning something new. Little did I know my four-year-old son, Garrett, would increase my insight of creating a personal vision. I signed Garrett in for class, gave him a hug, and said, "You are going to have an awesome day!" He responded with excitement, "See-ya, Dad," as he quickly dashed for the playground. Little kids were everywhere playing tag, swinging, yelling, and sliding down the giant red slide. The playground, at preschool, expanded my knowledge of persistence and practice to reach a vision.

Before leaving, I observed Garrett playing with his peers. Garrett ran to the big yellow monkey bars and waited in line behind four other preschoolers. Each student, one at a time, swung across laughing from one end of the monkey bars to the other end. I watched intensely as Garrett stepped up to take his turn. He grasped the first bar with two hands, hung on for a few seconds, and then let go. While watching from a distance, I called out, "You can do it Garrett!" He walked past the end of the monkey bars, looked up, and proceeded back to try again. Experiencing the same results as before, he continued to try again and again, without giving up, until the bell rang to line up for class. "See-ya, Garrett," I waved.

Each day, at preschool, Garrett practiced his skill on the monkey bars. One month later, while signing him in for class, Garrett pulled my arm and insisted we go to the playground together. "Watch this Dada," Garrett says, as he runs rapidly to the monkey bars to stand patiently in line. On his turn, Garrett gripped the first bar with one hand, anticipating the next bar with great momentum. He grabbed the second bar with a huge smile on his face. He continued to grab bar after bar after bar, smiling all the way; completing all bars in succession.

A child's persistence can teach us a lot. Garrett's mastery led him to teach his 3-year-old little brother, Galen, how to conquer the monkey bars. Often, I am observing life from a knee-high view. After watching my son, I learned that you must practice daily on the task you desire to accomplish, and smile your way through the process. Are there areas of your life you want to move forward and conquer? Set your focus on where you want to go and follow through with a heart of faith.

Life presents us with many opportunities to learn when we open our hearts to see.

Many people are searching for a personal vision. They are looking for meaning, direction, and a passion to achieve more in life. I believe Garrett saw himself accomplishing the monkey bars. His desire and persistence lead him to swing forward past other challenges. I believe a vision will push a person to achieve more than could possibly be imagined.

The Visionary

Have you ever watched someone operating in their vision? They have excitement and a purpose for living. When a visionary enters a room, the atmosphere reaches a new level. Recently, I was a guest on a national radio show talking about my first book, *Visualizing Your Victory*. Initially the host of the show planned to interview me for fifteen minutes, however, during the commercial break, he said, "Wil, I want to do an hour talk show with you." What turned a fifteen-minute interview into an hour? When I spoke, it was from my heart. I shared practical steps for creating a vision and reaching victory. The host stated "Wil, people are calling into the station requesting your book!" When vision connects with passion, people will notice you. You must bring energy and excitement to any environment.

Where there is no vision, there is no victory in life. Visionaries have the ability to see what is coming; while others, with a limited view of vision, will only see what is now. A visionless person only sees what is in front of them and believe their current position is their final position. These individuals have lost the ability for hope. Visionaries look forward to reaching positive and productive results. Faith is an anticipation of what you have already hoped for. What are you hoping for? Do you believe and know that all things are possible? I encourage people to believe and know that there is a brighter day ahead of them.

For many years I have mentored youth. One critical success factor in youth development is giving them a positive hope for the future. Without hope for the future, youth are more likely to engage in negative behaviors. Limited faith also leads youth to have minimal options. Many adults experience the same results when they lack the faith to reach for their vision. Developing the courage to go for a vision is difficult—however, worth it.

Sometimes life presents us with challenges and we do not understand why, only to push us in the direction we need to go.

Vision Blockers
Challenges will come and it may seem your vision is being delayed. When obstacles come in life, some people are destroyed and experience little hope. While others, when faced with adversity, develop an attitude of determination. People with a vision will breakthrough life's obstacles.

During a speaking engagement in 2005, I discussed vision builders and vision blockers. Vision blockers think and speak negative thoughts with attempts to destroy dreams, goals, or visions. Vision builders are people who dream of invisible things that will manifest into visible realities. A few days following the event, I received a call regarding my comments about vision blockers. The individual stated they identified themselves as being a vision blocker. They realized that their continual use of negative words towards their spouse had damaged their marriage of many years. My motivational speech impacted this person to let go of the vision block mentality and become a vision builder.

I have learned the steps of a vision: courage, anticipation, persistence, and an unmovable level of faith.

Vision to Victory

Are you taking action daily to reach your vision? Commit to moving one step closer to your vision today.

My senior year of high school was filled with many uncertain moments due to my academic performance. I remember sharing my goal of attending college with a group of peers. One individual in my peer circle said, "Why do you want to attend college? You will never make it. Give it up." Looking back on those negative comments, I am thankful I did not accept their comments. I chose not to allow negative comments limit my view or damage my dreams. When those bitter remarks were spoken, "You will never make it," I had a choice to make—accept or decline. I have met people that have allowed others' comments to tarnish their vision. Having a vision requires absolute faith and focus.

My college experience was a journey of proceeding from vision to victory. During my freshman orientation, a large group of students gathered in a gym to participate in the university's new student welcome. The guest speaker instructed all students to stand up, look in his direction, and then look to the right and left, and to the front again. He stated, "Some of you will not be here in two years, possibly the person on your right or left or maybe it will be you." I knew, in my heart, it would not be me.

In my second year of college, I was disqualified from the university as a result of low academic performance. Feeling down, I walked to the student union with the disqualified letter in my hand, sat in a chair, and placed my head on the table. I felt my vision of achieving a college degree was over. After a few minutes, a man approached me and said, "Is there something I can help you with?" I showed him my disqualification letter, and he asked me to walk to his office. Unknowingly, I was walking with the Vice President of Student Affairs. He invited the campus Ombudsperson to our meeting. They asked me about my college goals. They were impressed with my motivation to continue to move forward even with my current challenges. The Ombudsperson and Vice President of Student Affairs shared with me how I could be reinstated into the university by completing two summer school courses. I accepted their advice, successfully completed the summer courses, and was conditionally reinstated into the university. Three years later, I received my college degree. I am truly thankful for both the Ombudsperson and Vice President of Student Affairs for helping me reach my vision.

People are compelled to help you when you are committed to your dreams.

Vision Partnerships
A key to launching a vision is building effective partnerships. I have had the honor and opportunity of meeting many people worldwide. I know the importance of building valuable relationships with people. When you help others reach their vision, you will reach your vision. None of us can reach victory alone. From helping others reach their vision, I reached my vision by simply asking the questions, "What is your vision, and how can I help you?"

I conducted the first ever 24-hour Motivation teleconference at www.24hourmotivation.com on January 1, 2006. The call featured speakers from all over the world sharing their success stories and challenges while providing strategies to help individuals reach top performance. The teleconference reached over 27 countries and 28 states, and the many people who participated, as audience members, provided positive feedback, noting that the 24-hour Motivation teleconference had tremendously impacted their lives.

The success of this powerful call was a result of planting a vision and involving other people. From this vision, a successful harvest was produced. I am truly thankful that this vision is helping many people, worldwide, reach their potential, break through fear, increase profits, and build self confidence. What visions do you want to plant?

Every great idea starts in the heart of the one who believes.

The 9 Principles to an Abundant Vision
When I started on my vision journey, I developed confidence, commitment, and courage. I needed the courage to conquer my fears and lack of faith. I had to stop listening to my mind and follow my heart. In my mind, I was thinking of all the reasons why not to pursue my vision. Moving beyond the fears evoked nine principles that were critical and necessary for me to develop my powerful and purposeful vision.

The following principles led me to create a business in professional development and motivational speaking. I know these 9 principles will make a difference in all areas of your life.

#1 **Purpose**—Objective for searching for your vision. How will your vision add meaning to your life?

#2 **Passion**—Do what you enjoy and are excited about. At the beginning and end of the day what gives you satisfaction? List three things you are passionate about.

#3 **Potential**—Expand yourself to do more. Look at your life and challenge yourself.

#4 **Plant**—Use the gifts you have and find places to plant them. Plant them in the lives of other people. Who will your visions encourage? Watch success grow in others' lives.

#5 **People**—Find others that will encourage you to make your vision happen. List five people who will support your vision.

#6 **Process**—Understand that on the road to victory there are challenges. The process develops you.

#7 **Patience**—Great things will happen in your life if you focus on your anticipated accomplishments.

#8 **Position**—Place yourself in areas to meet and receive opportunities. List three places you will go to share your vision with others.

#9 **Produce**—Impact others with your vision. You are producing something on this path. Let it be known.

Your vision is a state of mind and being. Without vision people suffer from a lack of hope or spark of light. Life is dull without any excitement or anticipation of greatness. Use the nine principles as a blueprint to create your vision and accomplish your goals.

Your devoted desire to reach your vision will lead you to success. Have an anticipation to attract the right people that will assist you to reach victory. We all need others to help us achieve a vision. Continue to open your mind to new opportunities.

Now is the time for you to achieve the victory you deserve. What does it take to move from vision to victory? It takes ambition, determination, commitment, and a positive mental attitude—most of all, it takes you. I know there is a powerful vision inside of you. Your vision is filled with enormous potential. See what you want to accomplish, speak with confidence, surround yourself around vision builders, set your heart and mind to serve others on the vision journey, and set your standard for success. There is a vision builder within you.

You have the desire to go forward, no matter your condition, you clearly understand that you are in preparation for creating a better you, community, and world. Many people face obstacles and challenges, and they allow the adversity to become larger than the vision or they lose focus and look at their current situation and forget about their vision.

Check your heart condition—do you really want it?

Your heart must be pure for the vision to happen. Your vision will reveal how to make the life of others better by planting seeds of possibilities. I believe the major component to a thriving vision is helping others and including them in your vision. Remember, vision is the ability to see beyond where you are...and imagine your future possibilities.

Here are some necessary tips to maintain the momentum and move in the direction of your vision:

- When you connect to your vision, other people will benefit.
- Plant the vision in your heart. What is your heart speaking to you?
- What you put in your mind will produce a result. Think, meditate, and surround yourself around things that are positive.
- Who is in your circle of connection? Are the people in your life filling you up with encouragement or are they draining you with negative talk and actions.
- Develop a list of 10 power words that reflect your desire to reach your vision. Read your list everyday.
- Keep a vision log. Write down your thoughts, challenges, successes, and action steps.
- Have persistence. Your persistence will dismantle resistance. Refuse to accept defeat. You are victorious.
- Remember the monkey bars.

At the end of the day I will say:

I saw my vision.
I spoke about my vision.
I searched for my vision.
I served others on my vision journey.

Wil Cason, a man of meaning, has made it his life's work to provide others with the tools for success. Wil gained experience working in several diverse professional settings in the area of personal and organizational development. He released his first book, *Visualizing Your Victory* with visionpresspub.com in 2004. Wil shares his vision with others touring throughout the world speaking and giving weekly teleconference calls. Wil Cason currently resides with his wife and three children in Northern California, where he hosts his own motivational talk show, *Visualizing Your Victory*, every Sunday at 6pm PST on the web at www.jazzbeatradio.tv.

Chapter 12

The Power
Of a Mentor

Ruben Gonzales

Have you ever had someone tell you that you were destined to do great things in life? Did you buy into their belief in you? Sometimes we have to rely on someone else's belief until our own belief kicks in.

When Bob Mathias was young, he was an anemic, sickly kid. His love for sports drove him to get involved in track and field in high school. Over time, Bob developed into a solid all-around athlete, but he was not national level in any one event.

Four months before the 1948 Olympic Games, his track coach, Virgil Thomas, believed in Bob so much that he told him, "Bob, you have four years. If you got started right away, you could possibly make the 1952 Olympics in the decathlon."

Coach Thomas's belief in Mathias was incredible, because Mathias had never run the 1500 meters, he had never pole-vaulted, he had never thrown a javelin, and he had never even heard of the decathlon. To top it off, Mathias was only 17 years old!

Coach Thomas's belief was so strong that Mathias bought into it and started training right away. One month after he started training, Mathias competed in his first decathlon. Incredibly, he won first place! Two weeks later, he entered the U.S. Decathlon National Championship. He won again! Six weeks later, he was competing in the 1948 Summer Olympic Games. He had beaten his coach's prediction by four years!

Now Mathias was competing against much older and seasoned decathletes—the best in the world. Mathias amazed the world by becoming the youngest Decathlon Olympic Champion at the age of 17!

Someone asked him what he would do after his victory. Mathias said, "Start shaving." Mathias went on to win his second Olympic Decathlon in 1952. None of this would have been possible if his coach, his mentor, had not seen his greatness, believed in him, and encouraged him to pursue his dream.

When somebody compliments you, they have just seen a glimpse of your greatness. They have seen something about you that sticks out like a sore thumb. But it's so natural to you that you discount it.

Next time someone compliments you, thank them, and start using your outstanding gift to reach your dream. Surround yourself with winners, find a mentor who believes in you, and win the Olympic Gold in your personal and professional life!

Ruben Gonzalez is the author of the critically acclaimed book, "The Courage to Succeed." His experiences as a three-time Olympian, entrepreneur, and professional keynote speaker give him a unique perspective on how to conquer the corporate struggles of today. For his free 10-Part Success eCourse, visit **www.StartWinningMore.com** or contact him at (832) 689-8282.

Chapter 13

What I Know About a Pastor's Gift

Vince Gonzales

You may think it strange that you find a minister writing a chapter in a business or personal development book. The fact of the matter is—a pastor is a mentor. The dynamics that allow you to be an effective pastor are the same ones that will allow you to be a successful business person, executive, or a professional in any field.

There are certain foundational guidelines to follow that will allow anyone in any field to be successful and effective. What I know about the pastor's gift is exactly that—it is a gift. The first step to success is to discover your gift. You were created on purpose with a purpose. Every human being was created with a divine mission and purpose inside them. Just like everyone living was born with a heart and brain. You don't have to wonder if you have a heart, you know that you do.

Your purpose is just like that; it is standard equipment. The great new is when you discover that purpose, tagged right along with that is passion. Purpose and passion are like a rocket and jet fuel—passion, like jet fuel, will keep you flying.

The next thing you want to do is allow yourself to dream. Dream of things you desire, places you want to go, and things you want to accomplish. When you were a child, you had no problem dreaming. How do I know that? I talked with your school teacher. She told me you were always day dreaming in class!

Don't allow life, people, or circumstances to stop you from dreaming. Being a transplant patient, I know the challenge of keeping your dreams alive when life seems to be all uphill. I know the power of dreaming. Coming from a broken home and being heavily involved in gangs as a teenager, it did not seem like I had much of a future ahead of me. But then I had the good fortune of finding a few key mentors who helped me see the light, and realized I could do more and be more. They helped me build a dream for my future. From that small beginning, because I allowed myself to dream, I have spoken on the same platform with some of the top professional speakers in the motivational industry, become a published author, and most importantly, I have been able to share hope and love with hurting people. My advice to you is keep on dreaming and never stop.

The next step is to keep moving forward—especially when circumstances are yelling at you to quit. If you don't stop or give up, you will eventually meet a mentor who will help you get to your next destination on your journey of achievement. The old saying is true, "When the student is ready, the teacher will appear."

Listening is the next key to success. Hearing is the function of the ear; listening is a function of the heart. Many people do not need our words, they need our listening. Too many times when people talk to us, we are not listening, we are thinking about the things we are going to say next. Master the art of listening.

Which leads us to caring. People must know that we care about them. They cannot be just a dollar sign or a tool to get us gain. Back in the old days, many people approached sales in that fashion, looking at people as a big fat commission check. That is why in the back of the minds of millions of people, they hate salesmen! People want to know that you truly care about them.

Next, you want to learn to give people direction and guidance. People just want to be led. Your job is to share with them what to do, how to do it, and assist them to do it. The sale really begins after you get the check, not before. Make sure your definition of the word "sale" means service.

No matter if you are a leader, trainer, speaker, or in sales, give people one of the best gifts you can give them—hope. Hope is a powerful force, and if you want to reach your full potential, gives people hope.

The last part of success I want to share with you is balance. In a world where everything seems to be off balance, your job is to find the right mixture of dreams, goals, and responsibilities. Anytime you go after one area in the neglect of the others, you are sure to end up shipwrecked. Find the balance. It's the true measure of a successful life.

Vincent Gonzales is a dynamic young man with a true heart to help people grow in every area of their life. He lives in Southern California with his wife and two children. You can contact him at: vince@pillarsoffaith.com

Chapter 14

How to Stop Procrastination Starting Now!

By Mel Brodsky

Born to immigrant parents on a hot, steamy summer day in August of 1939, a child arrived into this world reeking of smiles, joy, and high expectations. Raised in an ethnic area of Newark, New Jersey, the families that settled there focused mainly on working real hard in order to save enough money to get their children to college, so that their children could have a better life than they had. I have to admit that most of the students in my high school did graduate, go on to college, and become professionals in their chosen field. I was one of the very few who not only didn't attend college, but I was actually invited to leave high school at the vulnerable age of 17.

I remember my Mom being asked to visit my teachers so often that when she didn't show up, they marked her absent. I can laugh about it now, but back then it was very humiliating, degrading, and painful. The other kids would be cruel and insensitive at times. That early trauma to a young impressionable mind seemed to set the tone for a good part of my formative years and way into manhood. A painful divorce, two children, and many broken promises later, I found myself alone, discouraged, broken hearted, and broke.

But wait! No need to feel sorry for me. My story has a happy ending. In the fall of 1971, I met a man by the name of Jim Rohn who changed my life and destiny, profoundly and permanently. This very wise, gifted teacher and mentor, through his philosophy, wisdom, and knowledge had the most remarkable ability to change people's lives, provided they were ready of course. I even thought back then, *what an incredible talent to possess, and how fortunate I am to have met him.* That was the day my life turned around and I was introduced to "The Power of Mentorship."

One of my biggest challenges back then and one I have to guard against to this day is the deadly "P" word—Procrastination. This infectious disease is the thief of opportunity. Procrastination will rob you blind, steal your bank account, and leave you destitute, discouraged, depressed, and eventually dependent on others for pity to take care of you. It took me many years before I finally got it. But by never quitting, persisting, and hanging in there, I finally got that monkey off my back! I now offer you what helped me defeat that formidable foe. Let's start with definition and clarity.

Procrastination: To put off or delay.
The Solution: Pro-action/Pro-activity.

Learn the law of inertia: "A body at rest tends to stay at rest; a body in motion tends to stay in motion." Motion leads to emotion. Emotion leads to action. Action leads to reaction and activity. Activity leads to results, success, fulfillment, self confidence, and self esteem. To illustrate this point, let me share what my very much alive one-hundred-year-old friend, Irene, said when I asked her what was the secret to a long, productive, and fruitful life? She became extremely animated and said, "You've got to keep the hands and feet moving at all times. You have to go, go, go. You can't slow down." Wow, what a colossal clue for living a full and extraordinary life—one of life's greatest lessons.

Let's explore why so many people procrastinate. Could it be fear? Fear of what? Failure perhaps? Success, rejection, or disappointment? Maybe the fear of being hurt or not feeling deserving enough? You pick the one or all of them that fit you. Why doesn't a person ask for a raise or promotion? Why doesn't a salesman make that sales call, and if he does, fails to follow up. Why doesn't a man ask a woman, that he has a great desire to know better, for a date? Why, why, why? Why is an orange not green? Because it is what it is—an orange. But, you and I are not oranges; we can change colors (habits). We have choices and options. Let's now determine what it's going to take to conquer procrastination, the nitty gritty.

#1 Reasons/Goals

One must have a strong enough desire, and unshakable "why to" in order to be victorious over this human struggle. Play the "What if?" game and ask yourself questions that will move you, provoke you to get off dead center and into momentum, and to do something different about the same old thing.

How will your life be dramatically altered when you deal with this deadly enemy of your hopes, dreams, and aspirations? For me, I was a nobody wanting to be a somebody, and I realized that my ambition would never be realized until I stomped that tyrant into oblivion! Ask yourself, *who am I and what do I want?*

Enter into a journey of self-exploration that will lead to a higher level of self-awareness, thus guiding you to optimum results and a very bright future.

#2 A Pro-active Plan of Action

Set yourself up for success by loading the deck in your favor. It starts by knowing thy self. Example: I have to watch myself like a hawk, because I'm very vulnerable to temptation and distractions. The only thing I can't resist is temptation, everything else I handle pretty well. It's just temptation that seems to follow me wherever I go. It's the T.V., the refrigerator, the telephone, etc. But here is where the rubber meets the road—it's how we deal with these challenges that will determine how our lives turn out.

Some of the things that have helped me are: I plan my day the day before. I find that daily goals are crucial to my success and productivity. I also, as best I can, plan my week the week before and for major projects. I work in 90-day increments; that seems to be the magic number.

Fill up your calendar meticulously and with purpose. Account for, and plan for, as many productive hours as possible to give yourself a specific direction, thus not giving procrastination an opportunity to rear its ugly head. Since many of these recommendations interface with time management skills, I like to use games and goals to keep me centered and focused. I use a personal time management assistant I call my "Time Genie" (compliments of my talented friend, "Action" Jack McClendon). Genie is an ordinary kitchen timer that follows me around in the course of my active day and, with my guidance, keeps my awareness of time at the forefront of my consciousness. Example: Even simple chores like the time I allot for myself in taking a shower in the morning, I could easily marinate in the shower for half an hour but that would not be in my best interest or time efficient. So I set my Time Genie for eight minutes and when the bell goes off—ding! I give myself an additional two minutes to wrap it up, thus practicing discipline and not giving procrastination an opportunity to dictate a part of my precious day. By the way, that's a savings of 20 minutes a day x 7 days a week x 52 weeks a year for a total savings of 7,280 extra minutes or 121 extra hours a year. That's 5 full days in this one small category!

You'll find yourself adding days, months, and years to your life while accomplishing and producing so much more. Genie is also an invaluable asset when gabbing on the telephone which can really be a time thief since it's so easy to lose track of time when lost in deep conversation with another. Depending on who I'm speaking with, I set her and forget her, but when my obedient servant calls me, it's time to terminate that segment of my valuable day and move forward.

#3 Affirmation—Confirmation Transformation Through Programmed Thinking

I strongly and fervently believe in affirmations because they have worked for me. But as my mentor reminds me, affirmations without discipline and action lead to delusion. You can't walk around all day proclaiming I'm thin and rich, I'm thin and rich, I'm thin and rich, and then go to the all-you-can-eat breakfast buffet on your way downtown to pick up your welfare or unemployment check. That's not the way it's set up. That's a recipe for disaster, disillusionment, and disappointment. I suggest starting with the truth with where you are now, where you want to go, and when you want to get there. If you're fat and broke, your mantra could be: I'm fat and broke but by year's end with desire and a game plan, I will be thin and rich! An affirmation I write, read, and affirm everyday is: "I am healthy, wealthy, wise, blessed, and grateful," and it's been so powerful, through this publication, it's brought me to you today.

#4 Spaced Repetition

Use this concept only if you have a strong desire to accelerate the learning and achieving process. I have learned a very expensive lesson over the years, and it has cost me dearly in time, money, and fractured relationships. My hope is to prevent it from happening to you. I've been a perpetual student of personal growth and development for the past 35 years and have been addicted to seminars, books, tapes, CDs, and videos on this subject for more than 3 decades. There was a costly, unsophisticated, and naïve major mistake though that I kept repeating. Although seminars, books, tapes, CDs, and videos got me very excited and gave me a momentary rush, I did not realize that listening or reading something just once was not nearly enough to really get it and absorb it. To this day, whenever I experience one of these life-changing vehicles, I get so excited and enthusiastic, you have to scrape me off the ceiling I'm so wired. I'll say, "That's it! Bingo! The missing ingredient!" But unless I put into practice spaced-repetition and application, the valuable information will abandon me like the "Elusive Butterfly of Love." The magic number to listen, read, or watch is 7 consecutive days. That will allow the wisdom, knowledge, and inspiration to penetrate your subconscious mind, and thus become part of your being and the new and improved person you're now evolving into. It's been said that it takes 21 days to break an old habit and replace it with a new one. You pick the number; you're the best judge of who you are. For me, seven is a great place to start.

#5 Balance—One of the Great Human Challenges of Our Time

It's not easy, but we must achieve it for a healthy, fulfilled, and well-rounded life's journey. To balance personal, economical, spiritual, social, recreational, and making time for family and friends is a juggling act that takes effort, awareness, desire, and skill—but the rewards are well worth it.

It's easy to lose sight and procrastinate when it comes to calling a time out from our active and stressful lives to plan a vacation or even a full weekend away from the maddening crowd, but is essential for living the good life. It starts with a desire to do it, and awareness that it's in you and your family's best interest and scheduling it on your calendar. This is a gift you deserve and owe to yourself. Trust me on this one. Just do it!!!

#6 Don't Try to Do It All by Yourself

Ask for God's help. This stuff is not easy; there's so much we have to unlearn. It takes time, effort, persistence, perseverance, and patience (it took me sixty six years to get here). I'm not a religious fanatic by any means, but it seems to me that the Bible is an excellent source and resource for learning about life. Your life! There are wonderful stories about people who have succeeded and failed that we can draw on to save us a lot of heartache, heartbreak, and time. What an invaluable "Instruction Manual" for life it provides. But even though God is good, God is not enough. Humans need other humans, to touch, to feel, to interact and share with. To laugh and cry together is such a profound gift in our lives for it warms the soul and soothes and heals our hearts.

We can also stop procrastination in its tracks using the value of teamwork and working with people we like respected and trust. The value of teamwork and healthy relationships is so crucial and vitally important to our well-being. "Snowflakes like human beings are two of nature's most fragile things, but just look what they can do, when they stick together."

In conclusion, I know and believe you can conquer procrastination starting now! All you need is a desire to get more out of life, a willingness to learn, change, and grow, and be fortunate enough to meet good teachers and mentors along the way, like the ones in this publication who help guide your path and make it fun.

Sincerely,

Mel Brodsky

P.S. Whatever I wish for myself, I wish you double!

Mel Brodsky is a talented and much in demand public speaker and trainer. He is the author of the bestselling book "Questions are the Answers." Mel can be contacted by phone at 888-909-8331 or email at mel@youvegotmel.com, or visit his website www.youvegotmel.com.

Chapter 15

The Power of Patience

Wanda Mattero

As I start my chapter on patience, I want to say it is not my intention to convert or offend anyone, but I just find it impossible to write on patience and leave out the one who gives us life, our Creator, God.

The definition of patience is: "To handle pain or difficult times calmly and without complaining." Most of us really struggle with this, and I used to be one of them. I was one of the most impatient people around, but I learned throughout my life, in order to be at peace with others and myself, I would need to change my way of thinking.

God is very kind and **patient** waiting for us to change. All of us, who struggle with impatience, need to change our way of thinking; we need to repent. The definition of repentance is: "to change one's mind," or "to feel sorrow, regret, or contrition for."

I have again found that patience and love are closely related. In 1 Corinthians: 13:4-7 the Apostle Paul writes: "Love is **patient** and kind and is not proud. Love is not rude, it is not selfish and does not get upset with others; love does not count up wrongs that have been done. Love is not happy with evil, but is happy with the truth. Love **patiently** accepts all things.

It always trusts, always hopes, and always remains strong." When we are impatient, we become angry, rude, sometimes hostile, complaining, and irritable.

Most of us really don't like what we become when we are impatient, and we defiantly are not listening to God. We actually become our own worst enemy. Impatient people get stressed out over the smallest circumstances. Being stressed will lead to an array of illnesses such as high blood pressure, ulcers, heart attack, and more. It will also cause the breakdown and death of marriage relationships and friendships.

Through the Holy Spirit we receive patience. The apostle Paul again states in Galatians 5:22, "the Holy Spirit produces the fruit of love, joy, peace, **patience,** kindness, goodness, faithfulness, gentleness, and self-control." When I started putting these teachings into practice, I found myself changing, and as I started to change, I looked at my life differently. Little things that used to irritate me didn't seem to bother me anymore. When I learned to let go and patiently wait on God's perfect timing, things started happening for the good in my life. I learned that all I had to do was ask for anything and I would receive. I have to admit there were times when it took a little longer than I wanted, but I also learned that everything happens in God's perfect timing. "All things work together for the good, for those who know the Lord, and are called according to His purpose." (Rom: 8:28)

Two years ago, I was put to one of the most trying tests of my life. At the time, I was going through this trial I wasn't sure if I would be able to endure it. If it were not for my faith in God, I know I would not have survived. It took a tremendous amount of strength and, yes, a tremendous amount of **patience**. I can honestly say if I had to go through it again, I would, because I came through it, not only victorious, but also closer to God than I have ever been. God has blessed me greatly and keeps on blessing me everyday.

Two years ago, I wrote a letter to my pastor and would like to share that letter with you.

May 19, 2004

Dear Pastor Joe,

I am the woman who talked to you after church last Sunday. I asked if it was okay to write you a letter. I wanted you to know how much the Lord has helped me by speaking through you these past few months. First, I would like to tell you a little about my background. I am the granddaughter of a Baptist minister on my father's side of my family. My grandparents lived in Oklahoma and were born in the late 1800's, before the first automobile. Grandpa was a traveling preacher. He did not have his own church, so he would go from town to town on horseback and preach the gospel.

Every year my dad, mom, sisters, and brother would go to Oklahoma to visit my grandparents. I have such fond memories of those vacations. My dad had twelve kids in his family, and all of them loved the Lord. My aunt once told me that my grandparents used to lie prostrate on the floor and cry out to the Lord for salvation of their children and children's children for generations to come, until our Lord returns. I have two cousins who are ministers and another cousin who is the wife of a minister.

I remember as a small child my family going to church together, and after church we would go visit my aunts and uncles. I loved those times in my life, but suddenly my dad stopped going to church. I don't know why, he just stopped. I became rebellious after that and had a difficult time in school. When I was thirteen years old, my family went on vacation to Idaho to visit my grandparents on my mom's side of the family. There was a revival in town (Boise, Idaho), and our entire family attended. I was so moved by what the pastor was saying that I accepted Jesus Christ into my heart. After we returned home, I strayed away from the Lord, but I know he never left me just like he promised, "I will never leave you nor forsake you;" (Hew 13:5) and I could always feel His presence.

I married at age 20 to a man I had only known for five months. He had a terrible drinking problem and was very abusive. We were married for 20 years, and during that time, I was belittled and abused verbally. I turned my life back to Jesus and started attending a Bible study, but the abuse at home just would not stop. Then my husband started threatening me with physical abuse, so I filed for divorce. After the divorce, I found myself out in a world I didn't know how to deal with. I had been a stay-at-home mom all those years and really did not know how to take care of myself.

I bought a condo and a hair salon thinking it would give me security in the future, boy was I wrong. Things started to go downhill from there. I really didn't know the first thing about running a hair salon, and was having a hard time just paying all my bills. I know now that it was because I did not have Jesus in the center of my life.

It was around that time I met my second husband. He didn't drink and was very kind, and I thought he was everything that I was looking for in a man. There was just one problem I thought was minor, but it was major. He was of a different faith. I tried to convince myself it didn't matter, big mistake!

Not long after we were married, I discovered that my condo had a very serious mold problem. I called my association and they had it tested. When I asked for the results of the test, they refused to give it to me saying the test results were in the hands of their attorneys, and when they were finished with them, they would give me the results.

I was forced to have my condo independently tested by another laboratory and found it was contaminated with very high levels of toxic mold. The association wanted to come in and do the remediation, but they wanted me to sign a form releasing them of all responsibility, before they would start the work. When I refused to sign the release, they refused to come in and do the work. So I had no choice and filed a lawsuit against them. My husband and I moved out of the condo, so I purchased a motor home as our new residence. I refinanced my condo, so we would have a place to live while the lawsuit continued. My husband had antibodies to the mold in his blood, so he also had a personal injury suit against the association. I was forced to pay for all attorney retainer fees and the payments on the motor home, because my husband claimed he was broke.

The trial date was drawing near. It was supposed to be the last of March, but was postponed. Last November 26, the day before Thanksgiving, my husband walked out on me. He had found another woman and she was pregnant with his child. I could not continue to stay in the motor home, as it was parked in front of his father's house. I could not stand to watch my husband come and go, so I had nowhere to go except back to my contaminated condo.

When I returned to my condo, it was such a mess. I stayed up all night crying and cleaning. I could not eat or sleep, all I could do was cry. Every night I would wake up every hour. I cried out to Jesus for help, and opened my Bible and started reading. I also could only get one station on my T.V.; it was a Christian station that was being broadcasted out of Arkansas. The pastor was preaching on the book of Job. I started going to your church at that time. I have missed only one Sunday since then. Every Sunday God speaks to me through you. I have rededicated myself to God and have vowed to never stray from Him again.

The week before Christmas I was up very early, so I started getting ready for Church. I was completely ready at around 6 a.m. As I was coming out of my bathroom, I tripped over my blow dryer cord, and fell and broke one of my ribs. I didn't make it to church that Sunday; instead I spent the morning in the hospital.

On Christmas day I was back in the hospital again. I thought I had pneumonia in my lung. While I was in the hospital, I called my husband thinking he should know that I was in the hospital. This is what he said, "I wish you well and Merry Christmas, and by the way, I am not going to make the house or the association payments anymore. I replied, "If you do not make the payments, I will lose the condo." He said, "He didn't care, because he had his personal injury lawsuit and he didn't care what happened to me."

I am a hair stylist and don't make a lot of money. If it were not for Jesus in my life, I don't know how I would have made it. I have a beautiful born-again sister and a lot of friends that have helped me financially. I have given everything over to God, and I am trusting in Him to take care of me and in doing so have seen miraculous changes in my life.

When I went back to the condo, my life was such a tangled mess. I knew there was only one person that could fix my life and that was God. I haven't been able to watch T.V for the past six months and only listen to my Christian tapes on my car radio, so I really do not know what is going on in the World right now. I have completely emerged myself in the Lord.

There is also very little furniture left in my condo, and I do not have a bed. I could not turn on my furnace, because it is contaminated with mold. But God provided me with an air mattress and a space heater to keep me warm. I had to change mold attorneys two months ago, as the attorney said there was a conflict of interest now that my husband and I were going through a divorce. I found a Christian attorney who has been my lifeline. My husband is trying to get half of my settlement. God only knows why he thinks he deserves it, we have only been married less than two years, and he is not on title to my property.

We went into mediation last month on the 27th of April; the association is buying back my condo for fair market value. My husband received 25 thousand for his personal injury lawsuit, but he is not happy. He has put a lien against my property. My divorce attorney said my husband is not entitled to anything. I have paid for everything. He has paid nothing. As of this writing, I only have $200 dollars in my account. All the money I have is in my condo. The association will be buying back my condo soon, and I will have nowhere to go. But I am trusting that God will show me the way, and I will follow Him wherever he leads me. I know now that wherever He leads will be right for me. I have lost almost everything, but I have gained so much more. I have my God and the assurance of my salvation, and He has so many wonderful things planned for me. Through Him all things are possible.

Thank You, Pastor Joe, for being the Godly man you are, and God Bless Calvary Laguna.

Yours in Christ,

Wanda Harrison Mattero

I also promised God that when He brought me out of this trial, I would give a portion of my settlement back to Him. On Sunday, July 4, 2004, I walked up to Pastor Joe and handed him a check. When he opened the envelope, he gave me a big smile and a high five. After I left the service, I went to my new apartment to sign the lease. When I asked how much the first and last months rent would be, I was told only $500 dollars. When I said how could that be, I was told that I only had to pay a deposit for my little dog, Maggie, that the first and last months rent were free. God was already giving it back to me, to this day the more I give the more I receive.

After I moved into my apartment, I had to sleep on an air mattress for a few more days, until my new furniture arrived. The first night I slept in my new bed (that was the first time I had slept in a bed for nine months). I looked around the room and smiled and just started thanking the Lord for saving me. Every night I would wake up very early in the morning and would be dreaming about the number 316. Every night I would have the same dream. I finally thought, yes, that's my apartment number—316. Then it dawned on me, John 3:16, "for God so loved the world that He gave his only begotten Son that whosoever believes in Him shall not perish but have everlasting life." I knew then that even my apartment had been hand picked by God. My daughter found me a golden plaque with the name John engraved on it, and I placed it on top of my apartment number. My apartment number reads: John 3:16.

I now have a lot of compassion for people who are cold and hungry, because I know what they are going through. I try to give to the missions for the homeless, and always give to a poor homeless person that I see on the street. The funny thing is it seems like the more I give I always get more back. If you give love, you will get back love. If you give kindness, you get back kindness. If you give compassion, you will also get back compassion. Whatever you give, you will get it back ten times over.

I had been in my apartment for about five months, and I was walking past the recreation room when I saw a nice man sitting on the sofa watching TV. I walked over to him, sat down on the sofa next to him, and introduced myself. As we were talking, he received a telephone call. I heard him say something to the person he was talking to about being patient. Then he turned to me and asked, "How would you rate yourself on a scale from 1 to 10 in patience?" I said without hesitation "a 10." Then he returned to the person on the phone and said, "I'm sitting next to a 10." After he finished his conversation, we started talking. There was just something about this man. He had the kindest eyes and was so soft spoken. He had a quality about him that just seemed to draw you to him like a magnet. He told me he was an author, a public speaker, and a mentor. He also saw something in me I did not know I possessed—my ability to write. He became my mentor and my best friend. His name is Mel Brodsky, author of "Questions are the Answers."

You May Contact Wanda at:
E-mail: wondrouswanda@aol.com
Phone: (949) 294-6770

Wanda Mattero graduated from Beauty College in 1967. She worked until her first child was born, and then quit to raise her family. In 1983, she returned to work. In 1987, she bought a hair salon in Laguna Hills, California, and sold it in 1994. She worked as a children's hair stylist for five years. She has written and published a children's book, "The Wondrous and Wanda-ful Wishes of Children," and is currently working on a series of children's books. She is also a public speaker. She is currently working as a cosmetology teacher at a beauty school in Southern California.

Chapter 16

Haven't Succeeded Yet? That's the Very Reason Why You Can't Quit!

Pete Urueta

Haven't succeeded yet? That's the very reason why not to quit. A phrase I have lived by after overcoming so many obstacles in my life. I would like to believe that someone or something in my past had tried to stop me from achieving greatness, but that wasn't the case. The obstacles in my past were more mental challenges then anything else.

Now at the age of 40, these obstacles have turned out to be the greatest blessings in disguise. They have been the very essence of my motivation and pulled me toward success. I found that challenges teach you how to fight for what you believe. My desire is to inspire persistency within you in order to overcome any obstacle or challenge you must face while reaching the level of success you want to achieve.

MY PAST LIFE

I really struggled within myself up to the age of 30, because I couldn't see myself becoming successful at anything. I felt so insecure for many years because of what I had experienced as a child growing up. As a result, many of the negative thought patterns in my mind had not allowed me to see my own true potential for success.

Have you ever wondered why you are who you are? Well, I did, and I used to ask myself questions such as, "Why did God make me this way?" or "Why am I who I am?" I was so unhappy within myself that I would question myself many times with these same questions, and I could never find the answer. For many years, I thought of myself as a nobody. It felt as if I had a weight at the bottom of my soul, and I was dragging it everywhere in life.

NEW CHANGE

At the age of 24, I experienced a new spiritual change. I had received the Lord, and it caused a new change and direction in the course of my life, which was the start of an exciting journey. With this new spiritual change, I knew if I wanted to have true success, God had to take precedence over my life. This was the foundation that stabilized my character and personality and gave me the security I had longed for all my life.

By the time I had reached age 30, I had jumped over a huge hurdle, and I was able to obtain my GED (high school equivalency diploma). Why was a GED such a huge accomplishment? Well, I wasn't really a bright student in school. I was frustrated, I thought I was dumb, my comprehension was low, and I wasn't motivated. I was held back in the third grade, and in the eighth grade, I was held back again.

The following school year, I was put on probation and eventually I was able to move up to the ninth grade. I didn't graduate from the ninth grade, but I did pass to the tenth grade. In high school, I completed the tenth grade with zero credits, and then I was transferred to a continuation school. After completing my first year there, I final ended school with only 39 credits. That was enough to drop out and I did.

After 12 years out of high school, I accomplished the impossible—I obtained my GED. I never thought I would ever accomplish this, because I had given up on getting my diploma. But, once I obtained my GED, I knew anything, and I mean anything, was possible now. WOW! What a victory. Something changed in my way of thinking. I remember asking myself the most empowering question ever. A question of perseverance, "If I could accomplish this, then what else can I accomplish?" Now I was really determined and challenged to succeed.

Although I have had many setbacks in the first three decades of my life and into my thirties, it has enabled me to develop a strong mindset, and as a result, I have learned how to be persistent. However, it hasn't been easy, but it has been worth every sweat and tear of my learning experience. With each new obstacle and challenge I face, I'm able to stand with confidence, because I know that I will learn through each experience, and I won't have to doubt myself any longer. I know who I am.

THE WHOLE WORLD IN OUR MINDS

Years later, I enrolled at the University of Phoenix. I was in a Humanities class, and we studied the life of Vincent Van Gogh. He was a painter who lived during the 19th century. I learned a lot about his life and the struggles he had experienced. He seemed to have struggled most of his life and even up to his death.

His life really helped me understand how he was able to see things in life differently than the average person during his time. Even though life seemed to have dealt him a bad hand, it seemed to have shaped his view of the world. In my opinion his perspective on life is what shaped his ability to express himself and paint in such a way he was considered a genius.

When I studied the life of Van Gogh, I made an interesting observation. We all have our share of struggles, some more then others. At times, when we go through these struggles in life, we look at them as something we do not want to face. It seems as if things have a way of just showing up at the wrong times in our lives, smacking us where it hurts, and it just doesn't seem fair.

What if our attitudes toward challenges allowed us to see them as something we could build upon? What if we took these challenges and allowed them to take root and shape our perspective so that the genius within each of us would be drawn out? What if we allowed the very things that hurts us the most, the fears we hate, and the trials we avoid, to change our attitudes? I believe we all have struggles, but the difference is in how we handle them. Will they make us or break us?

BAD DECISIONS

For so many years I felt like such a failure, thinking that the decisions I had made were really stupid. I've looked back and thought to myself, "If only I would have made the right decisions, things would have turned out better." Boy, did I feel like I made some regrettable decisions.

I look back now and believe that even though my decisions were not the best, at least I made decisions. I have taken what seemed negative and turned it into a positive. Now I can say that I would rather have made decisions and learned from those decisions than to never have made decisions at all. With wisdom and experience, I can make decisions and continue to make decisions when I see the right opportunities.

In my observation, the human reason gives us the ability to change perspectives toward certain experiences, just like my bad decisions. It seems as if God gave us the ability to use the intangible resources: reason, to change our perspective. We can change the direction of our course anytime we want, but it's not until we understand the tools within us that we can begin to start using them to help us in throwing off the weights that stop us from persevering toward the mark. It's when we learn to let go of the past, we can run the race without any hindrances.

BELIEVE IT BEFORE YOU SEE IT

I was in conversation with a friend of mine, who is in the same business as myself, and asked him a question. "If you could see into the future, and you knew after a year you were going to earn $100,000, would you take this business more serious?" He said, yes. Then I thought, if we knew without a shadow of a doubt we could be successful and it was crystal clear we were going to make it happen, we would probably be a lot more patient and not quit, knowing the end

155

result. It seems to me that most of us are not patient and aren't willing to see the results, because we don't see the evidence of our success.

It is easy to believe in something when it has already happened. It's easy to seclude ourselves from others; it's easy to lose; it's easy to complain; it's easy blame others; it's easy not to take responsibility for our own actions; it's easy not to decide, it's easy to follow the masses; it's easy to follow the opinions of others; it's easy to sin; but it's not easy to stick it out when success doesn't come immediately.

For me, I'm convinced of this one thing, if I don't care about my own success, then why should anyone else care; but if I do care about my own success, then others will care. I know there are people who don't want us to succeed, and we do need people who can challenge us. I believe if we are going to succeed, we need to associate ourselves with people who are willing to fight with us. People who are running the same race we are. I am talking about people who have been dashed against the rocks of life; people who have a win-win attitude; people to lock arms with us; and people who know everything about us and still want to be our friends.

GET UP AND FIGHT

Art Williams, in his book, PUSHING UP PEOPLE, writes, "I love the story of a runner, Glen Cunningham, because it exemplifies the kind of refusal to admit defeat that makes champions different from other people. Cunningham was in a terrible fire when he was only five. The doctors told his parents that the burns on his legs were so severe that he would never walk again. He would have to spend the rest of his life in a wheelchair.

But the doctors didn't know about Cunningham's determination. He vowed he would get out of bed and walk. And he did. He practiced constantly, using an old plow to hold himself up. Step by step, he dragged his legs along until they would move on their own. Once he was able to walk, he wanted to run.

And he did run, faster then anybody ever had, as a matter of fact. Cunningham went on to become a great mile runner, setting a world's record of 4.00.68 in 1934, and was named as the Outstanding Athlete of the Century at a celebration in New York.

How determined are you to win? How persistent are you to succeed? How many times are you willing to fall? The question is not, are you going to fall. The question is how many times are you willing to get up?

OUT OF THE LAND OF BONDAGE

In the Bible, God's people had been in bondage under the Egyptian government for 400 years. One day, God heard their cry and He positioned a leader by the name of Moses to deliver them from the hands of the Egyptians. After delivering the children of Israel from the land of Egypt, God brought them out and into the desert in order to cross over to the Promised Land, flowing with milk and honey. During their walk through the desert, God performed miracle after miracle, demonstrating His power and love toward the children of Israel.

However, they began to complain, complain, and complain. Instead of paying the price, walking in faith, and remembering what God had done for them, they wanted to go back to Egypt. They felt it would have been better to have continued in slavery and been ruled by the Egyptians than to travel through the desert where God would watch over them. They had forgotten about the bondage they were delivered from and what God had promised them.

I noticed similarities between people who give up in pursuit of success and the children of Israel. Even though we've been blessed with this land of opportunity, most of us become mentally enslaved by our own vises, not allowing us to reach our full potential in life. When most of us realize how dissatisfied we are with our current lifestyle, we decide to change once we feel tired of being stuck in a rut. From the land of bondage and into the desert, we realize the price is unbearable and then, slowly, our heads start turning back toward the land of bondage. How soon we forget how miserable we were and why we left Egypt in the first place.

When things haven't turned out the way we've wanted them to immediately, what do we do? We look back and complain, complain, complain. We soon forget and want to return to the lives we were living when it starts getting uncomfortable in the desert. We focus so much on the past that the promises waiting for us seem small compared to the price we have to pay.

It was this type of life I had lived for many, many years and to be honest with you, I hated it. There were many times I was on the road toward the Promised Land, and as soon as times were rough, I started to look back to the land of bondage, and eventually I returned. What if we could be patient because we knew the end result of all things? Would that have a different affect on how we would walk through the desert?

THE REASON NOT TO QUIT

I think life is too short not to take advantage of each and every opportunity that comes our way. Wouldn't you rather be on your death bed and say, "At least I tried," than never having tried at all? I usually tell my friends that I'd rather die trying than never have tried at all.

I don't believe there are any shortcuts in life. Either we do it or we don't. Either decide or don't decide. Either make it or don't make it. Either we live or we die. Either take action or don't take action. Get my point? There are no easy roads—just roads.

If I thought I had to be a millionaire before writing a chapter in this book, then I would have missed the opportunity. But guess what? I decided, pursued the opportunity, took action, and it was done. I believe persistence is one of the keys in attracting success. I'll worry about making my millions later, but for now I have written my chapter. So remember, the reason you're not successful is the reason why you should not quit.

Pete Urueta currently resides in Whittier, California, and is in the sales and network marketing industries. He has helped coach and mentor individuals from sales to spiritual matters.
Contact Information:
Phone: (562) 665-1911, Email: pete.urueta@adelphia.net,
Website: www.prepaidlegal.com/hub/urueta

Chapter 17

Books Are My Favorite Mentors

Charlie "Tremendous" Jones

Everyone who knows me knows my mentors are books. As a salesman, it was books; as a manager, it was books; in my home, it's books; with my friends' lives, it's books. Years ago I had a habit of giving everybody a book with my card. I hoped they were read, but if not, they were there to be read.

In his book, *You and Your Network*, my friend Fred Smith tells how Maxey Jarmon mentored him. I must admit that I felt a little envy as I read of their relationship. But when I thought of all my tremendous mentors in books, I think of myself as the most blessed man in the world.

I would like to share with you one of the greatest ideas you will ever hear.

A few simple changes in your daily routine can improve the quality of your life. From now on when you read a book, make the author your mentor and always read with your pen in your hand. As you get used to reading with a pen in your hand, you begin to cultivate the habit of making notes of things you actually think in addition to what you thought you read.

We must learn to read, but only to get our own minds in motion and start our thought processes.

I practice this in church. When the pastor starts to preach, I take out my pen and start making notes of things I think. This excites the pastor because he thinks I'm writing out his sermon. Sometimes I think he should throw away his sermon and use my notes. As I leave church I get a smile or laugh when I say, "Pastor, you were really good this morning. You interrupted my train of thought a half dozen times." Whether it is selling, preaching, or teaching, interrupting their train of thought to help them see what they know will always bring a smile or a laugh.

Fifty years ago I attended a lecture. I don't remember much of what the speaker said, but he made me laugh for an hour at my problems, as I identified with many principles that convinced me that even though we had never met, we were very much alike. As he closed his talk, he said, *"You are the same today that you will be five years from now except for two things—the people you meet and the books you read."* If you hang around achievers, you will be a better achiever; hang around thinkers and you will be a better thinker; hang around givers and you will be a better giver; but hang around a bunch of thumb-sucking complaining boneheads, and you will be a better thumb-sucking complaining bonehead. The "people you meet" and people you surround yourself with are your best mentors and a key influence in your life. We need mentors and positive role models as much as we need positive goals.

The trouble with our role models and heroes is that we can't take them home. We have got to grow and experience the lessons of life *alone*. But don't mistake aloneness for loneliness. Some people think they're lonely because they're young, while some people think they're lonely because they're old. Some people think they're lonely because they're poor, and yet some people think they're lonely because they're rich. Some discover that everybody is lonely to some degree, and that's the way it's supposed to be. You discover out of loneliness comes aloneness when you decide to live and grow. You alone decide to live your life and do your growing. No woman grows for a man. No man grows for a woman. No parent grows for a child. *When you grow, you grow alone.* Growing brings growing pains, but the laughs come too if humor is a part of your growing.

I mentioned "thinking with and listening and speaking to the heart," and about seeing things in perspective and learning to laugh at our growing pains, using humor to break down barriers in our own heart and between other people. But you will never realize these points in your everyday experience without the stimulus of reading that broadens your perspective and pulls you out of the negative cycles that can develop in your own thinking.

Here are some examples of my mentors in books.
General Patton made his troops mad and glad. He made them think and laugh when he wasn't around. General Patton once said, "If we're all thinking alike, somebody isn't thinking." When you're thinking, you're constantly discovering new dimensions to everything; when you're the wisest you know the least; and when you're aware of your ignorance, you're the wisest. How good it is to realize my ignorance. General Patton said not to be afraid of fear, "Fear is like taking a cold shower. When the water is ice cold, don't tip-toe in—

leap in and spread the pain around. *Success isn't how high you reach, success is how high you bounce every day when you hit bottom."* Patton almost always helped his listeners see with their hearts what he was saying.

Abraham Lincoln is one of my favorite mentors. His life has served as an inspiration to people from all walks of life. Many people will tell you that one of the secrets of excellence is education, yet Lincoln had little formal education. His family was so poor that for a period in Lincoln's childhood, they didn't have a door to their cabin. The year after his mother died, eight people lived in a small one-room log cabin. Many believe if you're raised in poverty or a broken home, you don't have much of a chance of growing beyond your past.

There's a lot of emphasis on self-esteem today, yet Lincoln had little reason to believe in himself. His mother died when he was a boy. He had little time with his hard-working father. His sister died when she was in her teens. The woman he married didn't make his life a bowl of cherries. There were very few people in Lincoln's life who were there to stand by him and offer him positive encouragement of what he could and should do.

So, how does a man who lacks most of the things that we say you should have to be a successful leader, become one of the most revered heroes of world history? Two of the many great assets of Lincoln were his ability to tell stories in order to illustrate a point and, while doing so, get people to laugh with him. Much of this was stored in his mind and heart through the book mentors he loved as a boy. Lincoln was a great thinker, because he learned to *read and laugh*.

I would be remiss if I talked about mentors and my philosophy, and I didn't mention my mentor Oswald Chambers. Nearly every word I have spoken for 50 years has been flavored by this man. Yet it's no small wonder that many have never heard his name, because Chambers died in 1917 at age 43. He never wrote a book. How can I have thirty of his books if he never wrote a book? He married the Prime Minister of England's secretary, and when he went to work with the YMCA in Egypt during World War I, she went with him and made shorthand notes of his talks. When he died in 1917, she lived on for years and wrote all the books from the notes she'd made.

Let me tell you why Chambers is my favorite mentor. He challenges my everyday thinking with a warmth that has grown out of the struggles of his own heart. He helps me see how wrong I am in a way that lets me laugh at myself. Chambers says, "You can determine how lazy you are *by how much inspiration and motivation you need to do something.* If you're for real, you do it whether you feel like it or not. The best way to avoid work is to talk about it."

Get people to think with you, and you'll get them thinking better. Get them laughing, but don't let them laugh *at you.* Some comedians get people to laugh at them. And sometimes being a clown is necessary to loosen things up. But good managers, teachers, and salespeople learn how to get people to laugh *at themselves.* You begin by seeing things in perspective and learning to laugh at your own situation.

I urge you to read and motivate others to read. *Never read to be smart, read to be real; never read to memorize, read to realize. And never read in order to learn more, as much as you read to re-evaluate what you already know. Never read a lot, but read just enough to keep hungry and curious, getting younger as you get older.*

Success for me is one word—thankfulness, learning to be thankful. The first mark of greatness is thankfulness: the first sign of smallness is thanklessness. An attitude of gratitude flavors everything you do. Once in a while some young tiger will say to me, "Did you feel this way years ago when you didn't have anything?" I used to go home and say, "Honey, look at me. "Man of the Month." Look at this, "Man of the Year." She would say, "Where's the cash?" I'd say, "Honey, if we don't start learning to be happy when we have nothing, we won't be happy when we have everything." Well, I don't know if I ever sold her, but I finally bought it myself. I'm not trying to sell you, I'm buying it myself and sharing it. The one great thought, more than any other, is to be more grateful and thankful.

When you are in the game and wrestling with problems and achieving goals, the natural tendency is to focus on you. But if you don't balance this with a perspective that realizes where other people are relative to you, with their needs and goals, and realize the simple joy of living and growing through the stages of life, then all your goals and involvement, whether they are successful or not, will only lead to bitterness. The heart of success is thankfulness. When your heart is in a thankless state, you can laugh, but not at yourself.

When my family sits down to eat, our giving thanks goes something like this, "Dear God, we thank you for our food, but if we had no food, we would want to thank you just the same. Because, God, we want you to know we're not thankful for just what you give us, we're thankful most of all for the privilege of just learning to be thankful."

Thank you for sharing my thoughts. I hope you were thinking with me and that someday we'll meet and you'll tell me I interrupted your train of thought several times. May my thoughts help you realize that there are no mentors like books.

Charlie "T" Jones, CPAE, RFC "Tremendous" Publisher-Motivator-Humorist Thousands of audiences around the world have experienced nonstop laughter as Mr. "T" shares his ideas about life's most challenging situations in business and at home. Two of his speeches, "The Price of Leadership" and "Where Does Leadership Begin?" have been enjoyed by millions. He is the author and editor of nine books, including *Life is Tremendous* with more than 2,000,000 copies in print in 12 languages. Visit his website at www.excutivebooks.com or call 800-233-2665.

Quick Order Form

The Power of Mentorship
By Don Boyer

Power of Mentorship ...$12.95

Shipping
$2.50 for first book
$1.25 for each additional book
(California residents add 8.25% sales taxes)

Fax Orders Send this form to: 562-945-5457	**Telephone Orders** Call Toll Free 1-866-871-4487 (Have Your Credit Card Ready)
Email Orders melindatavera@realifeteaching.com	

Name: _____

Address: _____

City/State/Zip: _____

Phone: _____

Email: _____

Method of payment: Visa or Master Card

Card number: _____

Name on Card: _____

Exp. Date_____   3-digit security code in

(If billing address is different from shipping addres